IMAGES
of America

WASHINGTON, D.C.'S
MAYFLOWER HOTEL

The description for this 1960s postcard for the Mayflower is still true today; it reads, "located in the heart of the Nation's Capital on Connecticut Avenue, convenient to the White House, Government buildings, Embassies and shopping." The sender wrote that he had not had much time for sightseeing but that President Eisenhower and FBI Director J. Edgar Hoover spoke at his convention. The Mayflower continues to be a place to witness history while in Washington, D.C.

ON THE COVER: The lobby of the Mayflower Hotel is shown on opening day, February 18, 1925. (Courtsey of the Mayflower Hotel archives.)

IMAGES
of America

WASHINGTON, D.C.'S
MAYFLOWER HOTEL

Keith McClinsey

ARCADIA
PUBLISHING

Published by Arcadia Publishing
Charleston, South Carolina

Library of Congress Catalog Card Number: 2007922160

For all general information contact Arcadia Publishing at:
Telephone 843-853-2070
Fax 843-853-0044
E-mail sales@arcadiapublishing.com
For customer service and orders:
Toll-Free 1-888-313-2665

Visit us on the Internet at www.arcadiapublishing.com

*To everyone who has worked at the Mayflower Hotel—their hard work
and dedication have made this hotel a national treasure.*

CONTENTS

ACKNOWLEDGMENTS

Thank you to the following individuals for their support and guidance before this project even began: Karen Finberg; Chris Madoo; Jill Keehner; the History Factor; Christian Mari, general manager of the Mayflower; my friends Linda Medalla and Lauren Carr for listening to me rant about history; and, especially, Frank Fleming, who worked at the Mayflower for over 40 years and cared more than any individual known to me about the history of the hotel.

There were three major resources for this project: *The Mayflower, Washington's Second Best Address*, written by Diana L. Bailey; *The Mayflower Hotel, Grande Dame of Washington, D.C.* by Judith R. Cohen; and most important, the anonymous writers of the *Mayflower Log*, the hotel's own publication for its first 50 years. Throughout the book, unless otherwise noted, all photographs are courtesy of the Mayflower Hotel. Much of what we know about who stayed and lived at the hotel and the events occurring there and around Washington can be found in the logs—they are a treasure! With over 80 years of history, it is impossible to tell the entire story of the Mayflower; hopefully this book will inspire those interested to learn more not only about the Mayflower but other historic hotels.

INTRODUCTION

Ground was broken for the Mayflower in July 1922 on a site that had earlier been occupied by the Visitation Convent and School and was at the time a most fashionable residential area of Washington, D.C. It was not an uneventful construction, as the excavation crew shortly discovered that an underground branch of Rock Creek ran directly under the hotel site. Further excavation revealed several ancient tree stumps, some more than eight feet across and estimated to be at least 100,000 years old.

The architect selected for the project was the New York firm of Warren and Wetmore, in association with the small Washington firm headed by R. F. Beresford. Warren and Wetmore were regarded as the premier designer of hotels in America. The firm's credits included the Plaza, Vanderbilt, Ritz-Carlton, Biltmore, and Commodore Hotels in New York. Perhaps its crowning achievement was New York's Grand Central Terminal. Robert Beresford was a government architect early in his career and later designed a number of private residences. He served a term as president of the Washington Metropolitan Chapter of the American Institute of Architects.

The Warren and Wetmore design is regarded as having provided a brilliant solution to the problem posed by the hotel's irregularly shaped site, a consequence of the L'Enfant city plan with it diagonal avenues. In the hands of lesser architects, the building might have been awkward, uncomfortable, or, at the very least, wasteful of precious land. Instead, the dramatic angle of the west facade, with its two curved towers, combined with the imposing yet carefully proportioned bulk of the hotel's north wing along De Sales Street, uses the site to spectacular advantage to generate an exaggerated grand perspective on Connecticut Avenue.

The hotel, to be the largest in Washington at the time, was conceived by prominent Washington developer Allen E. Walker, and it was initially called the Walker Hotel and Apartments. It was to cost the then unheard of total of $11 million. Unfortunately, overruns even beyond that cost, as well as construction delays, pushed Walker and his company, the Walker Investment Company, into financial disarray, and he was forced to sell controlling interest in the hotel a few months before it opened on February 18, 1925, to C. C. Mitchell, a principal in American Bond and Mortgage Company, one of the venture's major financial backers.

The new owners, seeking to convey the elegance and nobility of the capital's newest and finest hotel, changed the Walker Hotel's name to the Mayflower Hotel after the ship that landed at Plymouth Rock in 1620. In 1920, the country celebrated the 300th anniversary of the landing. The original purpose of the hotel was to provide the public with an elegant and well-appointed home away from home. It was equipped with 1,000 richly furnished rooms including 112 spacious suites, a block-long promenade, and glamorous and breathtaking function rooms.

When the hotel opened, the press carried the news that the building contained more gold leaf in its adornments than any other building in Washington after the Library of Congress. This was principally in the Grand Ballroom, the Chinese Room, and the Promenade. The apartment wing of the hotel housed high-ranking government officials and members of Congress.

On February 18, 1925, the official opening of the Mayflower was the occasion for much formal and informal entertaining. The Washington Chamber of Commerce held its annual banquet for 800 guests in the Grand Ballroom. The Presidential Dining Room was filled with throngs of several hundred guests who dined and danced to Vincent Lopez's jazz orchestra.

When President-elect Calvin Coolidge scheduled the Charity Inaugural Ballroom for March 4, 1925, at the just-opened Mayflower, he began a tradition of hosting presidential events that continues to this day. Presidents and politics have always been close to the life of the Mayflower Hotel. Following his election to the presidency in November, Herbert Hoover opened his office headquarters in the Mayflower to receive callers prior to his inauguration. Vice Pres. Charles Curtis resided at the Mayflower during the four years of the Hoover administration.

President-elect Franklin D. Roosevelt, preceding his inauguration, resided at the Mayflower. The entire Roosevelt family was with him, remaining there until they could move into the White House. For years, the National Democratic Headquarters occupied space on the second floor of the hotel, and it also has been the scene of important Republican Party gatherings.

Pres. Harry Truman told a Jefferson-Jackson Day dinner at the Mayflower in 1948, "I want to say that during the next four years there will be a Democrat in the White House, and you are looking at him!" After leaving the presidency, when in Washington, the former president and Mrs. Harry Truman and daughter Margaret occupied a suite that had been decorated especially for them.

Entertaining royalty and foreign dignitaries has always been an everyday affair at the Mayflower. The hotel has been continuously the scene of functions given by and for distinguished visitors from around the world.

The Mayflower has seen many changes to the interior of the hotel while the exterior has pretty much remained the same. The most dramatic was a 1960s renovation that included the installation of vinyl brocade wall covering over the rough plaster walls in the promenade. That same renovation also included the first major alteration of the lobby since the installation of air-conditioning in 1934. The most striking change was the wood-panel enclosure of the mezzanine and the installation of a modern dropped ceiling covering the skylight.

In 1982, the Mayflower began an extensive restoration to return it to its original appearance and a renovation that completely modernized its entire infrastructure and service areas. The lobby restoration uncovered the huge, 25-by-60-foot skylight covering most of the length of the lobby ceiling, reopened the mezzanine level with the Mayflower's original distinctive wrought-iron railing, and made visible the bas-relief frieze and gold ceiling medallion above the lobby elevators. In the hotel restaurant, two large murals by prominent muralist Edward Laning and his assistant Philip S. Read were rediscovered.

After these meticulous renovation efforts, the Mayflower Hotel was placed on the National Register of Historic Places in 1983 and recognized as a significant building worthy of protection. Less than 10 years later, the hotel was added to the National Trust's Historic Hotels of America. The trust identified the Mayflower as a hotel that had faithfully maintained its "historic integrity, architecture and ambience."

One

"THE FIFTH AVENUE OF WASHINGTON, D.C."

CONNECTICUT AVENUE. By the late 19th century, the nation's capital was already one of the nerve centers of the world. Lower Connecticut Avenue between Dupont Circle and Farragut Park had become an elegant thoroughfare lined with embassies, expensive apartment houses, and fine shops, known as "the Fifth Avenue of Washington." (Courtesy of the Washingtoniana Division, MLK Library.)

BRITISH LEGATION. When British minister Sir Edward Thornton built the first foreign-owned legation in Washington in 1872 at N Street and Connecticut Avenue, it was considered a remote location. One of the most important Second Empire buildings in the city, the British Legation, shown at left, served as both the residence of the minister and the offices for his government. Its location influenced the development of the area as the most elegant residential sector of Washington, and within 10 years, the area was the most exclusive residential section of the city. (Courtesy of the Washingtoniana Division, MLK Library.)

PHILLIPS ROW. Designed by Adolph Cluss, Phillips Row was one of the most fashionable addresses when it was built in 1878 on the southwest corner of Dupont Circle and Connecticut Avenue next to the British Legation. It was designed for Samuel Phillips, a prominent attorney who made his fortune in Washington's early horse-drawn streetcar company. By the late 1920s, the row had begun to deteriorate as a residence as commercial use encroached on the area. (Courtesy of the Washingtoniana Division, MLK Library.)

ALEXANDER GRAHAM BELL HOUSE. One of the most prominent private homes on lower Connecticut Avenue was built by Alexander Graham Bell in 1892 at 1331 Connecticut Avenue. His architects designed a Romanesque Revival house with a special wing for Bell to host his famous Wednesday Evenings, where Washington scientists would gather. Designed by Bell, the home also featured an early form of air-conditioning that lowered the temperature by 20 degrees in his office during Washington's hot summers.

SHEPHERD'S ROW. Designed around a corner tower, the three stone-faced houses of Shepherd's Row at K Street and Connecticut Avenue facing Farragut Park were originally owned by the governor of Washington, D.C., Alexander Shepherd, architect Adolph Cluss, and Hallet Kilbourn. All three amassed fortunes through real estate speculation in D.C. just after the Civil War. The houses, built in 1883, were a center for the Washington social scene for 50 years until they were converted to office use in the 1920s. They were replaced by one of the many undistinguished office buildings along K Street built in the 1960s. (Courtesy of the Washingtoniana Division, MLK Library.)

2Y. Connecticut Avenue, Washington D. C.

THE ACADEMY OF THE VISITATION. Although the Georgetown Convent of the Visitation had been in existence for many years, the Washington Academy of the Visitation began as a separate institution in 1850 through the efforts of Fr. William Matthews of St. Patrick's Catholic Church. Seven nuns came to Washington in 1850 to operate a Catholic grammar school. In 1876, the sisters purchased seven acres of land on Connecticut Avenue between L and M Streets for $53,000. They opened a new street through the center of this block named DeSales Street after their founder, St. Frances DeSales. Always a poor convent, the sisters were able to support their school and themselves by selling parts of their four-acre tract north of the academy between 1877 and 1919. (Courtesy of the Washingtoniana Division, MLK Library.)

13

THE ACADEMY OF THE VISITATION. The Academy of the Visitation building was designed by Adolph Cluss, one of the most prominent Washington architects of the latter half of the 19th century. His design consisted of three massive pavilions connected by three-story ranges. The central pavilion was the most prominent with four full stories. Located here were the chapel and the principal reception rooms. The left pavilion was used for a student dormitory and classrooms, and the nuns lived in the right. The sisters sold their property in 1919 for the site of the Mayflower Hotel and with the funds were able to purchase 64 acres of land at 9001 Old Georgetown Road in Bethesda for a new cloistered convent. After their move, the order became strictly contemplative. (Courtesy of the Washingtoniana Division, MLK Library.)

STONELEIGH COURT. Built in 1902 at a cost of $600,000 by Secretary of State John Hay as a personal investment, the Stoneleigh Court at L Street and Connecticut Avenue housed many of the city's social and political elite. During the Depression, all of the large apartments were subdivided and the high ceilings lowered to conserve fuel. At the time it was razed in 1965, the building had been converted entirely into office use. (Courtesy of the Washingtoniana Division, MLK Library.)

THE ROCHAMBEAU APARTMENT. The Rochambeau Apartment House at 815 Connecticut Avenue was constructed in 1903, when the intersection of Connecticut Avenue and K Street was still prime residential real estate. It was one of the many examples of Beaux Arts architecture in Washington. With the establishment of the many New Deal agencies during the administration of Pres. Franklin D. Roosevelt came a shortage of office space. The federal government leased a number of apartment houses for office space, including the Rochambeau, which was occupied by various government agencies until it was razed in 1962.

AERIAL OF CONNECTICUT AVENUE NEIGHBORHOOD. This early-1920s aerial picture shows the strong commercial redevelopment of Connecticut Avenue between Farragut Park (bottom of the picture) and Dupont Circle (top left). The street and much of the neighborhood retain their tree-lined appearance, which would quickly change with the widening of Connecticut Avenue to accommodate the new electric streetcars. St. Matthew's Cathedral dominates the area as one of the tallest buildings in the center of the picture, but that was changing quickly as well.

Construction of the present St. Matthew's church began in 1893. The first mass was celebrated on June 2, 1895. The church was dedicated in 1913 and designated a cathedral in 1939 when the Archdiocese of Washington was established. The cathedral was designed by noted New York architect C. Grant La Farge in the form of a Latin cross and seats about 1,000 persons. Pres. John F. Kennedy's funeral mass was held at the cathedral on November 25, 1963.

Church of
the Covenant.
Washington, D. C.

THE CHURCH OF THE COVENANT. The Church of the Covenant at N Street and Connecticut Avenue was the most socially prestigious of all Presbyterian churches in Washington and was attended by so many secretaries of state that it was sometimes referred to as "The Church of the Government." During the 1950s, when membership declined because of the flight of residents to the suburbs, plans were made to build a new church away from the encroaching commercial district. The statue of Presbyterian minister John Witherspoon still remains in the small island created at Connecticut Avenue and Eighteenth Street. Church leaders argued that the statue should be moved to their new location; however, the federal government countered that the statue was placed there with permission of Congress and could not be moved without an act of Congress. (Courtesy of the Washingtoniana Division, MLK Library.)

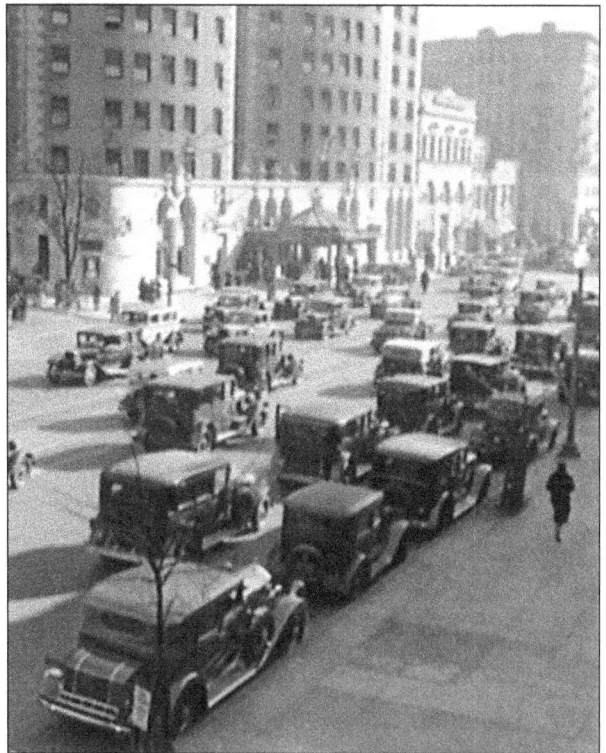

CONNECTICUT AVENUE. The early 1930s were a time of great prosperity in Washington, D.C. Lower Connecticut Avenue outside the Mayflower was becoming a busy area in the city as visible by the numerous cars on the street. (Courtesy of the Library of Congress, Prints and Photographs Division, Theodor Horydczak.)

METRO CONSTRUCTION ON CONNECTICUT AVENUE. In this February 1972 picture, construction islands line Connecticut Avenue as work begins on the city's famed Metro system. According to newspapers of the time, overnight construction in front of the Mayflower was limited so as not to disturb the hotel guests. Additionally, the construction team put mufflers on the cranes and bulldozer and had the sidewalks swept clean regularly. (Courtesy of the Washingtoniana Division, MLK Library.)

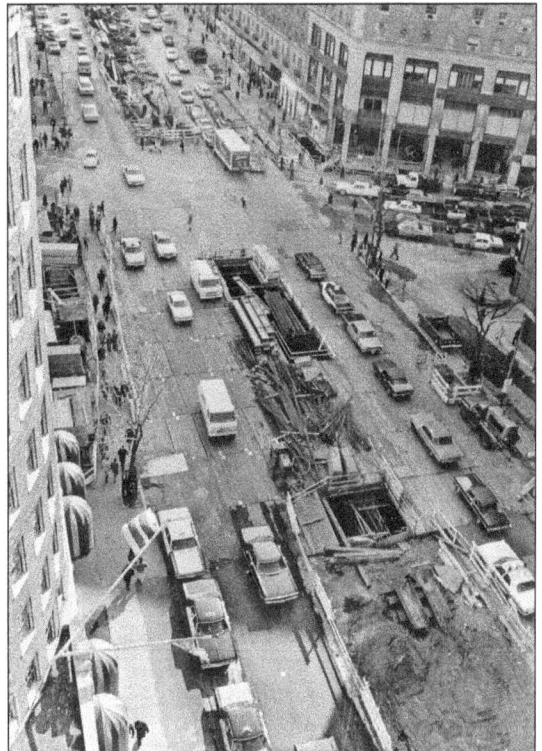

METRO CONSTRUCTION ON CONNECTICUT AVENUE. Taken from the roof of the Mayflower Hotel, construction of the metro followed a system of cutting a hole in the street and then covering the area once construction was complete. This method saved money but was very disruptive to both the street and pedestrian traffic as construction moved through the city. (Courtesy of the Washingtoniana Division, MLK Library.)

COMMERCIAL DEVELOPMENT OF CONNECTICUT AVENUE. Following the completion of the Metro construction in the early 1970s, Connecticut Avenue began the final phase of razing the last remaining historic brownstones, apartment buildings, and early commercial buildings between Dupont Circle and Farragut Park. These were replaced by modern office buildings, each resembling the other as more and more began to line the street. (Courtesy of the Washingtoniana Division, MLK Library.)

AERIAL OF CONNECTICUT AVENUE. As seen in this aerial picture, the neighborhood around the Mayflower Hotel is located between Dupont Circle in the center and Farragut Square at the top, three blocks from the White House. This area is centrally located in downtown Washington, D.C. Connecticut Avenue was one of the original streets in Pierre L'Enfant's plan for Washington and continues today to be a busy shopping and dining area. (Courtesy of the Washingtoniana Division, MLK Library.)

Two

THE MAYFLOWER
SETS SAIL
1925–1933

HOTEL UNDER CONSTRUCTION. Six months after the opening of the Mayflower Hotel, seen here under construction, came the addition of a million-dollar annex. The annex featured the presidential and vice presidential suites. Each of the state apartments consisted of a 13-room residential unit offering a foyer, drawing room, library, secretary's room, dining room, and five bedrooms each with a bath, kitchen, and maid's room. At street level, the Mayflower Coffee Shop was expanded.

WALKER HOTEL AND APARTMENTS BROCHURES. District developer and builder Allan Walker envisioned creating an elegant, European-style hotel to be called the Walker Hotel and Apartments. He selected a site just four blocks from the White House, and using designs from Robert Beresford and the firm of Warren and Wetmore, ground was broken in 1922. The Beaux Arts structure was masterfully constructed on the trapezoid-shaped plot at Connecticut Avenue and De Sales Street.

MAYFLOWER HOTEL BOND. Building costs exceeded $11 million because of the discovery of an ancient swamp beneath the hotel grounds. In August 1922, workers digging the foundation ran across huge cypress stumps, some measuring more than 8 feet in diameter. Geologists pronounced the stumps at least 100,000 years old, according to a report by scientists of the Geological Survey and John Hopkins University. With debts mounting, Allan Walker was forced to turn over controlling interest of the Walker Hotel to the American Bond and Mortgage Company. Walker died suddenly of a heart attack in May 1925.

MAYFLOWER ADVERTISEMENT. The new owners, seeking to convey the elegance and nobility of the capital's newest and finest hotel, changed the Walker Hotel's name to the Mayflower Hotel. This followed the national celebration in 1920 of the 300th anniversary of the *Mayflower*'s 1620 landing at Plymouth Rock. The image of the ship has been used throughout the hotel, on the front of brochures, and in works of art that adorn the building.

The Mayflower

Connecticut Avenue, midway between The White House & Dupont Circle.

Washington, D.C.

Permanent home of Statesmen Diplomats and Society

Lobbies and Public rooms artificially cooled in summer

VISITORS *to the Nation's Capital after the middle of February, will enjoy the maximum of comfort at The Mayflower, Washington's newest and finest hotel.* ∞ ∞ ∞ *Advance reservations now being accepted.*

HERE *you will find rich beauty and intimate refinements to please the most discriminating patron* ∞ *A real welcome awaits you, and no effort will be spared to make you feel at home.*

Telephone Main 9800

Cable Address Mayflower

CONNECTICUT AVENUE

De Sales and Seventeenth Streets, Northwest.

LOBBY. The main lobby of the Mayflower, on Connecticut Avenue, stretches the entire length of the hotel, 475 feet to Seventeenth Street. On opening day, it was described as an example of dignified elegance, luxurious but in no sense ornate. The most striking features of the lobby other then the skylight are the four great bronze torcheres, hand wrought and trimmed with gold and said to be almost priceless.

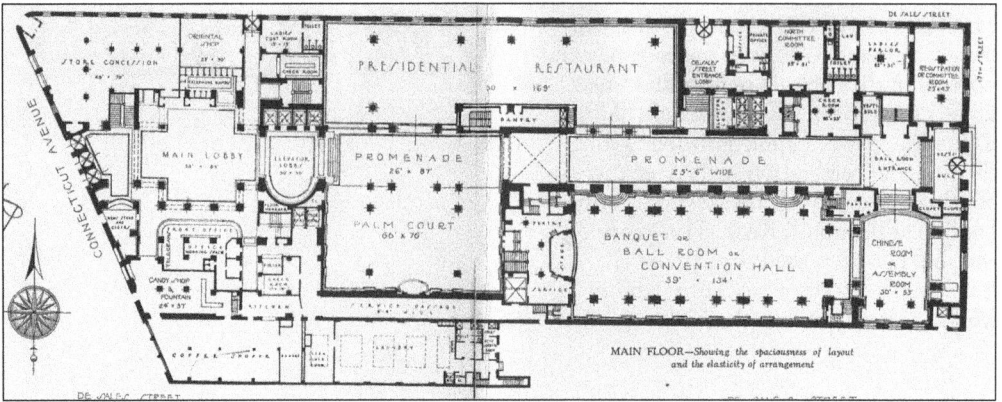

MAYFLOWER FLOOR PLAN. Almost three acres of space were devoted to public use. The first two floors contained a restaurant, coffee shop, the Palm Court, private banquet, and writing rooms. One level below the lobby was a grill room.

GARDEN TERRACE. Beneath the main floor was the Garden Terrace. This room featured a coppered ceiling, a large dance floor, marble fountain, and landscape murals of Washington and Mount Vernon. The atmosphere suggested the outdoors, with warmly tinted high plaster walls and alcoves that looked like latticed arbors. This room more than any other in the hotel has changed the most over the years.

PROMENADE. Merging into the lobby is the Gallery or Promenade. The stretch of the Promenade was designed to hold a collection of art, fine antiques, and draperies. At one time, the Promenade included two Louis XIV gold consoles over which hung large mirrors, three Aubusson tapestries made in France in the 18th century, and several commodes. Most impressive were three statuaries: *The Lost Pleiad* by Randolph Rogers, *La Sirene* by Denes Puech, and *Flora* by Cooper Williams. Unfortunately, these were sold in 1948 to the national Memorial Park in Falls Church, Virginia.

25

GRAND BALLROOM. An exquisite entertainment salon, the Grand Ballroom was equipped with a disappearing stage and silver screen, with room for large assemblies, balls, conventions, musicals, and lectures. The room was painted in ivory, gold, and vermilion. It had a vaulted ceiling, black-and-gold marble pillars, lush gilt ornamentation, and murals painted by Venetian artist Ampelio Tonilio. Balcony boxes lined three sides, including the Presidential Box used during inaugural balls.

CHINESE ROOM. Inspired by Whistler's famous Peacock Room, the Chinese Room was decorated in glowing reds and blues of the Chinese Chippendale style. With gleaming lacquer, sumptuous hangings, and mural decorations in the Oriental gilt, this was considered an impressive and beautiful salon. It was reserved for receptions, teas, luncheons, and small meetings.

PALM COURT. The Palm Court, to the right of the Promenade just after the lobby, was opened to host tea dances during Prohibition. It was a great latticed room banked with palms and featured a beautiful marble fountain and pool with water plants growing in it. The centerpiece of the room was a large glass dome. After the repeal of Prohibition, the Palm Court became the Mayflower Lounge.

PRESIDENTIAL RESTAURANT. The Presidential Restaurant was the main restaurant of the hotel. This room had a stately, patriotic feeling thanks to the coats of arms from the various states and the portraits of the first four presidents. China and silverware bearing the image of the Mayflower finished the details of this room.

SEMI-HOUSEKEEPING BROCHURE. Over the years, guests have enjoyed the convenience services offered at the Mayflower such as an apothecary, florist, barbershop, hairdresser and manicurist, laundry, physician, broker, notary public, theater tickets, and sightseeing tours. The goal of Mayflower service was stated in this brochure: "service is a natural outgrowth of a standard that does not tolerate the merest suggestion of mediocrity. . . . it is dedicated to the single purpose of the comfort of the guest."

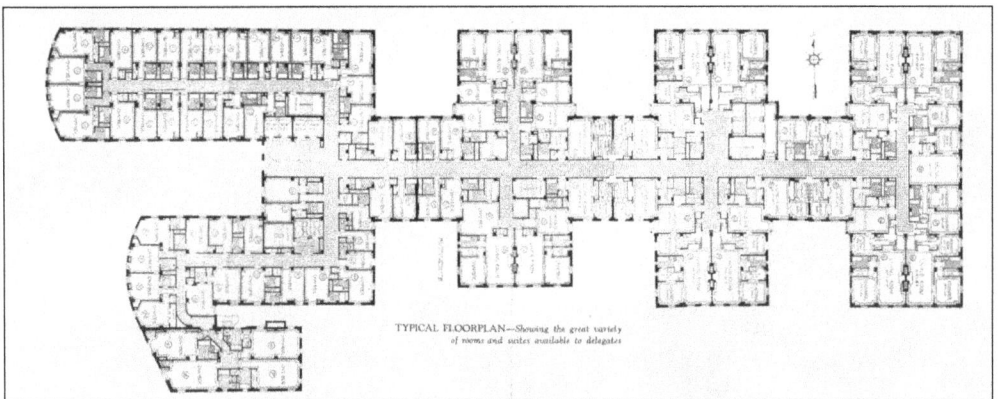

TYPICAL FLOORPLAN—Showing the great variety of rooms and suites available to delegates

GUEST ROOM FLOOR PLAN. The Mayflower was constructed as a 1,000-room hotel including 112 semi-housekeeping suites. According to an early brochure, the hotel was constructed with equipment and appointments to be the last word in hotel enterprise. In luxury of furnishings, cuisine, and the high quality of service, the Mayflower had become world famous.

RESIDENTS ENTRANCE. More than 100 of the hotel's original rooms were lush apartments. "Residents" were frequently federal government officials or visiting foreign diplomats who require long-term accommodations. Special guests enjoy a separate entrance and elevator located on De Sales Street with services including private desk clerks, bellboys, and doormen.

LIVING ROOM OF SUITE. The standard suite featured a large living room, dressing closet, breakfast room, and small kitchen, as well as multiple bedrooms and bathrooms. There were also smaller suites consisting of a living room with two beds that fold into a bed closet, a roomy dressing closet, bathroom, and breakfast room with kitchenette.

LIVING ROOM OF SUITE. Suites cost about $18 per day in 1925 and were designed so that no two were alike; each was given carefully chosen individual furniture with a special interest in grace, beauty, and refinement and in careful harmony with the color scheme of the room according to an early brochure on the semi-housekeeping apartments.

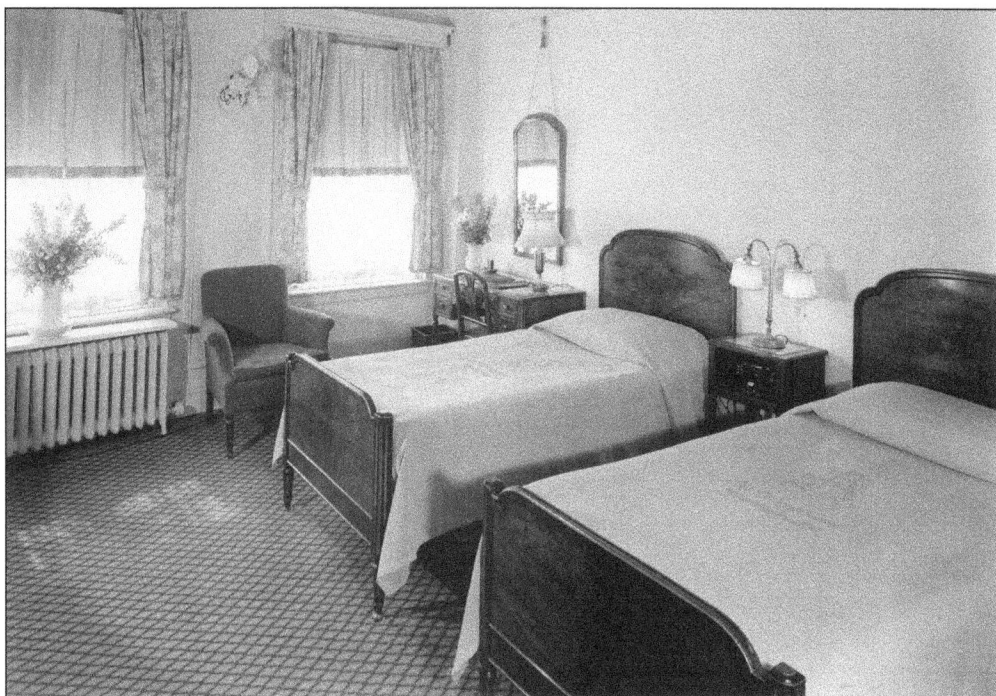

STANDARD GUEST ROOM. This early standard guest room with double beds for two people began at $7 per day, and there was an additional charge of $2 per day for each extra person. Each room featured the finest box springs and mattresses, oscillating fans, and ventilated closets and was designed to cater to the physical comfort of the guest.

BATHROOM. Each of the guest rooms featured their own bathroom, which during this time was considered a luxury in some hotels.

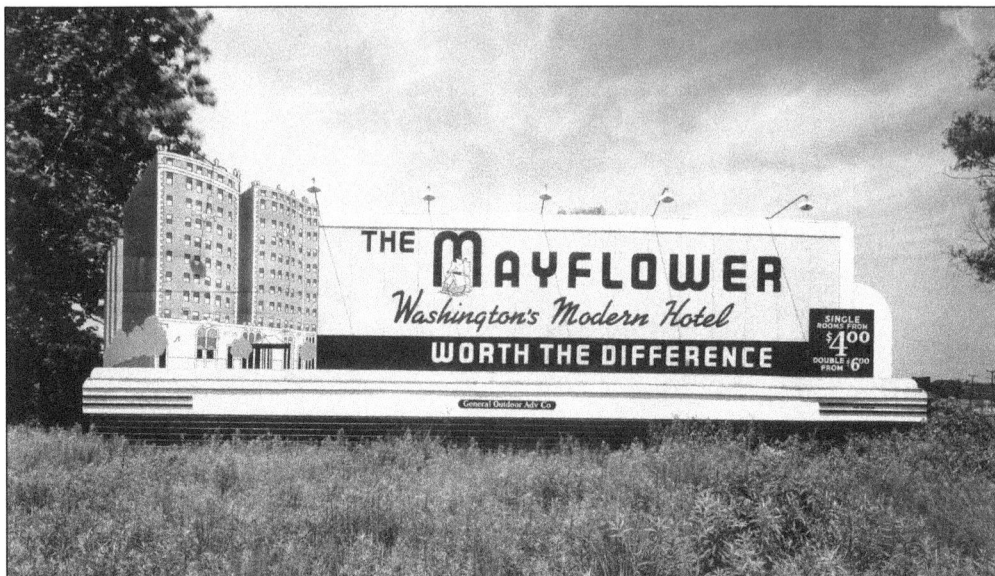

BILLBOARD, 1920S. This billboard advertised the Mayflower as "Washington's Modern Hotel" that proved to be "worth the difference." By 1932, there were 23 members of Congress living at the Mayflower.

Silently

AIR CONDITIONED BEDROOMS AT WASHINGTON'S MODERN HOTEL . . . . . . *Assure Healthful Sleep and Escape From All Outside Noises*

Restaurants ❖ Lobbies ❖ Public Assembly Rooms Also Made Delightfully Comfortable By The Quiet Flow Of Fresh, Washed Air . . .

Naturally Ventilated Bedrooms and Suites On Every Floor, If Preferred . . .

Single Rooms from $4 ❖ Double Rooms from $6 *All with bath, of course*

The Air Conditioned MAYFLOWER
WASHINGTON, D. C.
R. L. POLLIO, Manager
NEW YORK OFFICE
521 Fifth Avenue   MUrray Hill 6-2363

WEBSTER AIR WASHER. Air-conditioning was an early feature at the Mayflower Hotel—a rarity, since only movie theaters and large department stores had such conveniences in the 1920s and 1930s. During the hot days of summer, guests at the Mayflower Hotel could rest easy thanks to an early air-cooling system called the "Webster Air Washer." Located in the sub-basement, the apparatus worked by washing and chilling the air and then delivering it to the entire first floor and to a garden below.

DINNER PROGRAM. Although the first major social event occurred in March, the Mayflower Hotel actually opened in February with a dinner for those who helped design, construct, equip, and financially support the hotel. Among the 750 guests in the Grand Ballroom, honored guests and speakers included Secretary of Labor James J. Davis; Cuno H. Rudolph, president of the District Commissioners; Mr. and Mrs. Robert Beresford, architect of the hotel; Mr. and Mrs. George N. Vanderbilt; and the Honorable Albert D. Ritchie, governor of Maryland.

LOBBY OPENING DAY. The first full day of business was February 18, 1925. According to the *Washington Post*, the Mayflower was the largest hotel or private building ever erected in Washington at that time. The new hotel represented an investment of $11 million and covered an area of one and a half acres. The public was invited to the opening ceremonies.

MAJ. H. R. LEMLY. The first person to sign the Mayflower guest register was Maj. H. R. Lemly, a retired U.S. soldier and scholar. At the time of his move, he had already been a resident of Washington for over 14 years. Lemly had been around the world twice and spoke French, German, Italian, Spanish, Portuguese, and even some Japanese and Chinese. He was also fluent in Russian, which he learned while living in St. Petersburg, Russia. He was a noted collector of Oriental and Russian curios, and his collection had many famous pieces.

CALVIN COOLIDGE'S INAUGURAL BALL. The first major social event at the Mayflower Hotel was Calvin Coolidge's 1925 charity and inaugural ball. Although Coolidge did not attend because of the death of his 16-year-old son, 6,000 people showed up to dine and dance in the Grand Ballroom. Their efforts raised $40,000 for regional charities.

MAYFLOWER LOG. The hotel's own publication, the *Mayflower Log*, was launched on March 1, 1925. For the next 50 years, subscribers enjoyed monthly news about who stayed at the hotel and the events occurring there and around the District, as well as fashion tidbits, stories and poetry, and advertisements.

MAYFLOWER ORCHESTRA. Sidney Seidenman was a famous conductor and violinist whose orchestra entertained guests at the Mayflower Hotel for 41 years, beginning in 1926. On any given night, Sidney had orchestras playing all over the city, but he could almost always be found at the Mayflower. For many years, Sidney shaped Washington's social scene and was loved for knowing the classics as well as the most popular tunes. If someone asked for a song he did not know, he would send someone to find the music.

FLOWER SHOP. Since it opened in 1925, the flower shop has been a popular service at the Mayflower Hotel. During the 1920s, the *Mayflower Log* encouraged Washington hostesses to consult the Mayflower florist before entertaining, promising that the "reputation and responsibility of Washington's Finest Hotel accompanies every delivery."

INTERNATIONAL PARLIAMENTARY UNION MEETING. In 1929, the Mayflower booked its first large convention, a meeting of the International Parliamentary Union. In preparing for the meeting and anticipating the mass arrival of its guests, three baggage clerks were dispatched to New York to transport the luggage to D.C. En route, the clerks methodically tagged each of the bags with its intended room number. Additionally, the *Mayflower Log* printed a special version in Spanish and one of the meeting rooms in the Mayflower was renamed the Pan American Room.

AMERICAN LAW INSTITUTE. The American Law Institute first met at the Mayflower in April 1925. The *Mayflower Log* reported that the meeting was attended by eminent members of the legal profession from all parts of the country; the highlight was a banquet in the Grand Ballroom attended by nearly 500 people. Justice Harlan F. Stone was the presiding officer. After 80 years, the American Law Institute still meets at the Mayflower.

CHARLES LINDBERGH BREAKFAST. In June 1927, Charles Lindbergh celebrated the success of his historic nonstop flight from New York to Paris at the Mayflower Hotel. Breakfast for 1,000 was served. During his stay in Washington, D.C., he was awarded the Hubbard Medal by the National Geographic Society.

AMELIA EARHART. Following her solo flight from Newfoundland to the British Isles, Amelia Earhart posed in her Mayflower Hotel suite in July 1932 for a photograph by Underwood and Underwood Studio. Earhart, the first woman to cross the Atlantic Ocean alone, was in Washington, D.C., to receive the Special Gold Medal of the National Geographic Society from Pres. Herbert Hoover.

PRES. HERBERT HOOVER. After his election in 1928, Pres. Herbert Hoover declared the Mayflower his temporary headquarters in planning his administration before the 1929 presidential inauguration, spending 90 days in residence at the hotel.

VICE PRES. CHARLES CURTIS. During the Hoover administration, Vice Pres. Charles Curtis leased the Vice Presidential Suite on the 10th floor of the hotel during his term between 1929 and 1932. A widower, Curtis shared the 10-room suite with his sister, Mrs. Edward Everett Gann, and her husband. Mrs. Gann served as the hostess of her brother's apartment, which became the unofficial social gathering place of the Hoover administration.

WASHINGTON TIMES

Telephone District 5260   SATURDAY, DECEMBER 27, 1930   Office Address, 1317-21 H St. N. W.

Mayflower Hotel Feeds Unemployed

CHEWNING   POLLIO

MACK   O'BRIEN

CONVERTING a garage near its kitchens into a restaurant, the Mayflower Hotel is serving free meals daily to unemployed persons who are certified by the Salvation Army. Daniel J. O'Brien, president and managing director of the hotel, who inaugurated the plan, is shown serving mashed potatoes, and R. L. Pollio, resident manager, is handing out coffee, while C. J. Mack, chief accountant, and William Jeffries Chewning, Jr., well known in society circles and a member of the hotel staff, assist in the feeding of the line of jobless.

—Times Staff Photo

WASHINGTON TIMES. Daniel O'Brien, first president and general manager of the Mayflower Hotel, approached the Salvation Army in January 1931 to find out how the Mayflower Hotel could help the city's unemployed. A lack of wholesome meals was mentioned, and Mayflower staff rose to the challenge by opening a canteen nearby where people could get a good meal over the noon hour. Hotel guests were asked to donate any clothing to the cause that was no long of use to them.

WASHINGTON BALL. For the 200th anniversary of the birth of George Washington, a costume ball was held at the Mayflower and featured hundreds of guests as characters from history, including Pocahontas, passengers from the *Mayflower*, and, of course, George and Martha Washington.

George Washington Bicentennial Ball

given under the auspices of the

United States George Washington Bicentennial Commission

on Monday, February 22nd, 1932

at ten o'clock in the evening

Mayflower Hotel

Washington, D.C.

BACHELORS' COTILLION. Beginning in December 1928, the Bachelors' Cotillion provided prominent young women with the opportunity to be presented to Washington, D.C., society. A captive audience of prominent local bachelors ensured that the young ladies had ample dance partners. The December event was followed by cotillions in January and February.

Three

THE ROOSEVELT YEARS AND WORLD WAR II
1933–1945

EXTERIOR OF THE MAYFLOWER. Like so many other American businesses during the Depression, the Mayflower eventually joined the other hotels that went into bankruptcy because they could not meet their mortgage payments. In July 1931, its management was taken over by court-appointed receivers, who controlled it until June 1934, when it was returned to its original owner under Pres. Franklin Roosevelt's Corporate Reorganization Act.

OFFICE OF THE
COLLECTOR OF TAXES, DISTRICT OF COLUMBIA

Nº 1

RECEIPT FOR

ALCOHOLIC BEVERAGE LICENSE FEE

Feb. 6, 1934
Washington, D. C. _____ 193_

RECEIVED of _The Mayflower Hotel_____ 1127 Conn ave_____
                              NAME   ADDRESS

the sum of $___1,000.00_____ for a __Retailers_____License, Class__C__

for a_____Hotel_____ under the District of Columbia Alcoholic Beverage

Control Act.

THIS IS A RECEIPT, NOT A LICENSE

FILE WITH APPLICATION FOR LICENSE

ALCOHOLIC BEVERAGE LICENSE FEE. The 18th Amendment banning alcoholic beverages began in 1919. The Mayflower played a role in ending Prohibition by serving as the meeting place for the Women's Organization for National Prohibition Reform. The hotel was also the site of a critical meeting of the Democratic National Committee, which was the turning point in the repeal process in 1931. Finally after 14 long, dry years, Prohibition ended and the Mayflower quickly paid its $1,000 fee for a liquor license.

MEN'S BAR. Located in the front of the hotel with an entrance directly on Connecticut Avenue and another from the lobby, the Men's Bar was a favorite meeting spot of Washington men and would remain restricted for at least another 10 years. Women would continue to enjoy the elaborate afternoon teas in the Palm Court.

MAYFLOWER SILVER SERVICE. As the Mayflower's silverware superintendent, Fred Gleim made sure the table service was as attractive as the food served on it. Gleim started in 1934 and brought his son Howard on board in 1936. Working from the sub-basement, Gleim received flatware, coffeepots, teapots, and trays each week for polishing, repair, or re-plating.

COFFEEPOTS. Mayflower silversmith Fred Gleim would watch when parties ended so that things "won't walk away." He would keep count on the pieces, 150 coffee pots for example. He commented that teaspoons "don't stick around long" and that about 4,000 spoons, featuring the *Mayflower* ship engraved on the handles, have left the hotel. The strangest disappearance was a five-gallon punch bowl from a Christmas party.

SUITE 776. Elected president in 1932, Franklin D. Roosevelt occupied room 776 on March 3, 1933, the eve of his inaugural address. In this room, the new president penned one of the most famous lines in U.S. political history and reassured a nation gripped by economic depression by stating, "The only thing we have to fear is fear itself." More than 250 radio stations broadcast his message across the country. Suite 776 had been selected by the president on every visit to Washington.

PRES. FRANKLIN D. ROOSEVELT. Large crowds would always greet the president whenever he emerged from the Mayflower. The 1933 inaugural events were in March of that year; however, for President Roosevelt's second term, the date was changed to January 20, a change made by the 20th Amendment to the Constitution that continues today.

FDR BIRTHDAY. Some of the more memorable presidential affairs at the Mayflower were Pres. Franklin Roosevelt's birthday galas. Each year on January 30, FDR celebrated his birthday by holding a series of balls to raise money for childhood polio, a disease that afflicted the president himself.

OLIVIA DE HAVILAND. A personal friend of the Roosevelts, Olivia De Haviland was a regular guest at the president's birthday celebration. De Haviland was a two-time Academy Award–winning actress and was most famous for her role in *Gone With the Wind.*

AL JOLSON. A smiling Al Jolson (left) arrives at the Mayflower as master of ceremonies for Pres. Franklin D. Roosevelt's 1943 birthday ball. Al Jolson was an acclaimed singer and actor who is best known for his appearance in one of the first talking films, *The Jazz Singer.* President Roosevelt was unable to attend his own birthday celebration that year, but several celebrities were in attendance.

JAMES CAGNEY. General Manager C. J. Mack greets James Cagney arriving at the Mayflower during the 1940s for a black-tie event. James Cagney was an actor most remembered for playing gangsters in crime films.

MARY MARTIN IN THE LOBBY. Mary Martin poses in the lobby of the Mayflower for photographers. Mary Martin was a Tony Award–winning Broadway star and was famous for originating the roles of Nellie Forbush in *South Pacific*, Maria in *The Sound of Music*, and Peter Pan. She was a Kennedy Center Honoree in 1989.

ELEANOR ROOSEVELT. First Lady Eleanor Roosevelt was a social activist and firm supporter of her husband, Franklin Delano Roosevelt, who was U.S. president from 1933 to 1945. She personally selected their apartments at the Mayflower prior to moving into the White House. In January, Eleanor made a hurried inspection of the Mayflower and walked to the White House to meet with Lt. Col. U. S. Grant III, director of Public Buildings and Public Parks of the National Capital, concerning renovations to be made at the White House. She returned to the Mayflower in a taxi.

DANCE IN THE GRAND BALLROOM. The Grand Ballroom at the Mayflower was host to many college dances and proms, including this one from 1937. With a little over two years before the outbreak of World War II with the German invasion of Poland, the tuxedos would soon be replaced with military uniforms.

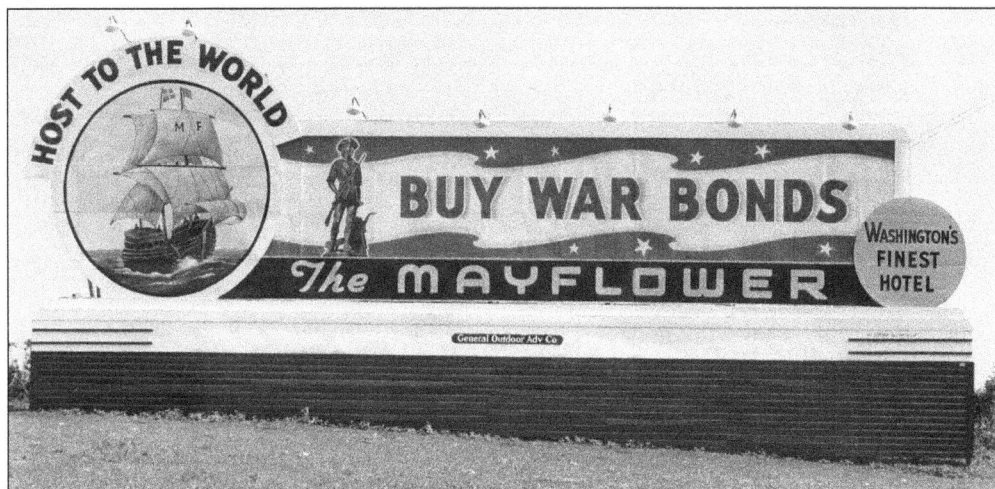

MAYFLOWER BILLBOARD, 1940s. The Mayflower Hotel contributed to the World War II effort in a variety of ways: The building was prepared for potential air raids, staff learned first aid, hotel billboards and publications encouraged the purchase of war bonds, and the hotel hosted numerous USO and fund-raising events.

MRS. ROOSEVELT. During World War II, Eleanor Roosevelt took an active role in promoting the sale of savings and war bonds as well as defense stamps. In September 1941, the Mayflower Hotel hosted the Retailers for Defense Week and was one of 6,000 hotels across the country to sell the stamps.

MAYFLOWER LOUNGE. The Palm Court became the Mayflower Lounge on April 2, 1934, and was renovated at a cost of $45,000. During World War II, it became Washington's most famous meeting place for Allied government and military officials. Table tents reminded guests to discuss any confidential war matters in hushed tones, as you never knew who was listening.

INTERIM CLUB. During wartime shortages, when people often arrived early only to find their rooms not yet vacated, the Mayflower opened an Interim Club. The club consisted of private closets, dressing rooms, telephone booths, and two attendants. The club allowed guests to freshen up, change their clothes, do paperwork, make phone calls, and receive messages and telegrams before their scheduled appointments. There was no charge for these facilities.

WALT DISNEY AND CLARE BOOTH LUCE. Walt Disney discusses his upcoming movie, *Victory Through Air Power*, with Clare Booth Luce in the lobby of the Mayflower Hotel. The U.S. Army contracted for most of the Disney Studio's facilities and had the staff create training and instructional films for the military, as well as homefront morale-boosting shorts such as *Der Fuehrer's Face* and the feature film *Victory Through Air Power* in 1943.

WORLD WAR II USO SHOW. Red Skelton (left), Marlene Dietrich, and George Murphy (right) chat between shows during one of the many benefits held at the Mayflower during World War II. Most of these events were held in the Grand Ballroom because of the number of people who wished to attend, and usually it was standing room only.

PRIME MINISTER WINSTON CHURCHILL. According to Mayflower legend, the acoustics in the Chinese Room played a trick on Prime Minister Winston Churchill in 1945. While attending a state dinner, Churchill leaned over to his neighbor to tell him an off-color joke. To Churchill's surprise, his voice was carried up to the dome and magnified, to the horror of two distinguished women and Pres. Franklin Delano Roosevelt, who were seated in the room.

GEN. CHARLES DE GAULLE. The Mayflower was a center of activity during World War II as heads of state often stayed here during visits with Pres. Franklin D. Roosevelt. Here General de Gaulle of France is seen arriving at the Mayflower on official business.

USO Dance and Canteen. The Grand Ballroom was host to many USO dances during the war. The USO was founded in 1941 in response to a request from Pres. Franklin D. Roosevelt to provide morale and recreation services to uniformed military personnel. USO centers and clubs opened around the world as a "Home Away from Home" for the GIs. The USO brought Hollywood celebrities and volunteer entertainers to perform for the troops. At its high point in 1944, the USO had more than 3,000 clubs, and curtains were rising on USO shows 700 times a day. From 1941 to 1947, the USO presented more than 400,000 performances, featuring entertainers such as Bing Crosby, Judy Garland, Frank Sinatra, Marlene Dietrich, James Cagney, Al Jolson, the Andrews Sisters, Lucille Ball, Glenn Miller, and, most famously, Bob Hope.

War Bond Benefit. Van Johnson and Gene Kelly (shown left to right at the microphone) entertain a standing-room-only crowd in the Grand Ballroom during a war bond benefit. Standing by the piano is Sidney Seidenman, the leader of the Mayflower Orchestra.

ORCHIDS AND CHAMPAGNE. The "Incomparable Hildegarde" performed at the Mayflower Hotel lounge during the Orchids and Champagne Party in 1941. An annual event, the Champagne and Orchids Party kicked off the fall social season for the Mayflower Hotel and the larger Washington, D.C., area. The event was usually held in October and had the tradition of presenting each lady with a beautiful purple orchid corsage as she arrived.

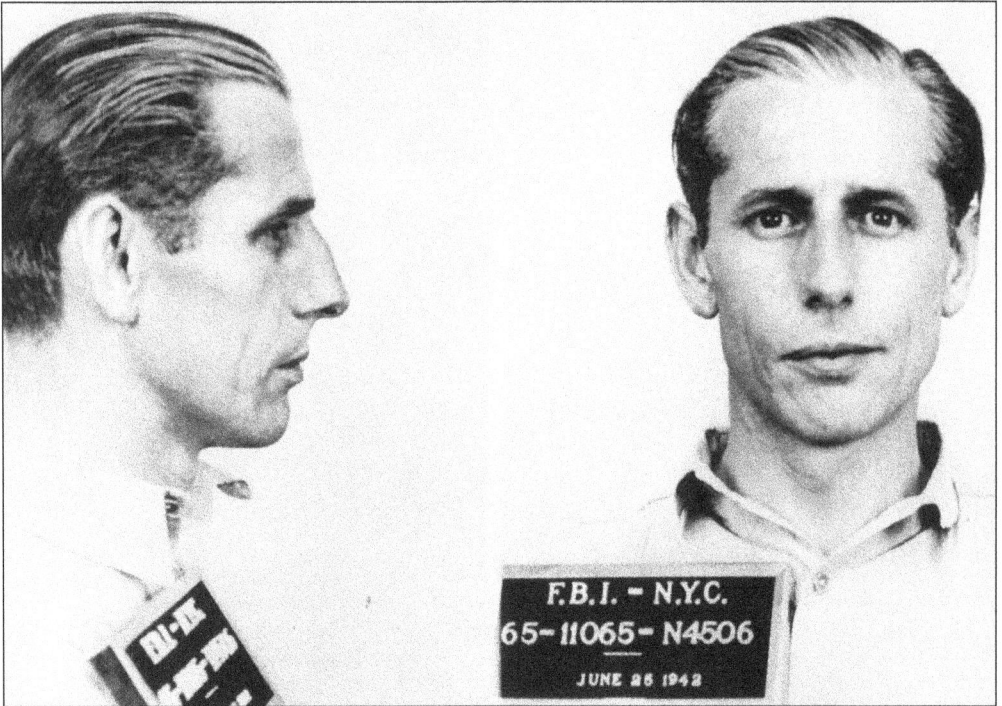

SPY AT THE MAYFLOWER. George Dasch was considered one of the most dangerous spies and saboteurs during World War II. In June 1942, Dasch and seven other Germans landed on America's shores and buried explosives with the intent to destroy U.S. factories and power plants. Dasch fled to Washington, D.C., checking in to room 351 at the Mayflower Hotel, where he contacted the FBI and revealed the saboteurs' plot. FBI operatives interrogated and incarcerated George Dasch at the hotel for over two days. George Dasch, as the informer, was sentenced to 30 years in prison, another saboteur was given a life term, and six others were executed.

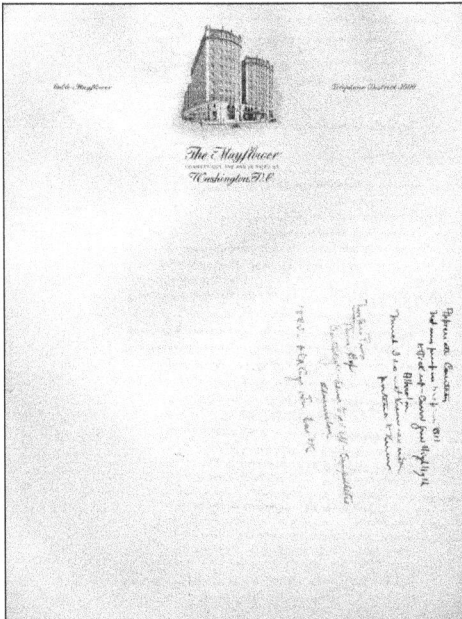

GI BILL. Harry Colmery, World War I veteran and former commander of the American Legion, pens a draft of the Serviceman's Readjustment Act, or GI Bill, on hotel letterhead here in 1943. Once passed, the bill assisted millions of veterans by helping to pay for their education or home purchase once they returned from war. In 2002, Colmery was posthumously awarded the Presidential Medal of Freedom.

Four

WASHINGTON'S SECOND BEST ADDRESS

1945–1960

THE MAYFLOWER HOTEL ENTRANCE. The Mayflower Hotel strives to provide the finest services to its guests the moment they walk through the door. Following World War II, it was business as usual with Mike Mann at his post as he had always been during his 42 years of service at the hotel.

MAYFLOWER CHEF. Nicholas Marchitelli was executive chef at the Mayflower beginning in 1930. He actually started at the hotel two weeks before it opened as assistant chef. He was trained as a cook in Italy, and his largest event at the Mayflower was serving 3,800 people at one banquet. His biggest satisfaction was the fact there was never a dish asked for that he wasn't able to prepare.

MAYFLOWER KITCHEN. Like the day it opened, the Mayflower Hotel has been abuzz with activity, much of it occurring behind the scenes. Seen here preparing a meal for a banquet, Chef Nicholas Marchitelli provided leadership and supervised all culinary activities during his years at the hotel.

BUFFET DISPLAY. Splendid food and luxurious rooms were not enough. Over the years, the banquet staff has delighted guests with lavish buffet displays for their reception. Most of the items pictured are from the hotel's inventory of silver and gold service, including custom tableware featuring a basket of mayflowers. This made sure the table was as attractive as the food served on it. Dinnerware was made expressly for the Mayflower Hotel, first by Black Knight/Hutschenreuther in Bavaria from 1925 to 1939. After the start of World War II, from 1940 to 1972, Buffalo China U.S.A and Shenango China U.S.A. provided "distinctive china for distinguished hotels," including the Mayflower.

MAYFLOWER WEDDING. The beautiful setting of the Grand Ballroom has been the backdrop for many weddings. The hotel provides the perfect space for large and small weddings that often include elaborate ceremonies, receptions, and dancing. In years past, the editor of the *Mayflower Log* frequently included descriptions of the bride's dress and other details about the reception.

NIMITZ DAY DINNER. Adm. Chester William Nimitz was the commander in chief of Pacific Forces for the U.S. and Allied forces during World War II and was America's last surviving fleet admiral. On September 2, 1945, Nimitz signed for the United States when Japan formally surrendered on board the *Missouri* in Tokyo Bay. On October 5, 1945, which had been officially designated Nimitz Day in Washington, D.C., Admiral Nimitz was personally presented a Gold Star in lieu of the third Distinguished Service Medal by the president.

JEFFERSON-JACKSON DAY DINNER. With the war over in 1948, incumbent president Harry S. Truman declared at a Jefferson-Jackson Day dinner, "I want to say that during the next four years there will be a Democrat in the White House, and you are looking at him." After leaving the White House, Pres. Harry Truman gave the hotel its tagline, "Washington's Second Best Address."

PRES. HARRY S. TRUMAN. This 1953 Democratic fund-raiser was held in the Chinese Room at the Mayflower with President Truman as the keynote speaker. The golf service centerpiece with fruit was apparently a favorite of the president's, and whenever possible, this piece was used on his head table.

HILTON HOTEL. In 1947, Conrad Hilton paid $2.6 million for controlling interest in the Mayflower by purchasing 200,000 shares of the common stock at $13 a share. Hilton was president of the Hilton Corporation, and the Mayflower was to be the 14th hotel in the Hilton chain. As soon as government regulations permitted, he promised a program of modernization of the Mayflower.

HILTON ADVERTISEMENT. This early Hilton advertisement shows the lobby of the Mayflower exactly as it appears even today. By this time, the Mayflower was only 25 years old but famous, as it says, "as a host to prominent people and as the scene of many internationally important events." Hilton would create many beautifully drawn illustrations of the hotel, some in color.

THE MAYFLOWER LOUNGE. September 11, 1947, was the opening of the newly remodeled lounge, the first phase in the Hilton Hotels Corporation program for "rehabilitation" of the Mayflower. Gone were the warm earth-color schemes, soft comfortable chairs, water fountains, and the openness of the room. They were replaced by chilling grays and blacks, uncushioned chairs, stark draped walls, and a totally closed entrance replacing the glass frontage. It was a complete failure aesthetically and financially and only lasted a couple of years.

RENOVATION SIGN. Again the Mayflower Lounge was closed for improvements, this time as a reaction to the Hilton modernization. While not totally recapturing the spirit and the feel it once possessed, the Mayflower Lounge would be more comfortable and the unofficial boycott would end. While work was proceeding, luncheons, cocktails, and dancing were provided in the East Room. Once reopened, the Mayflower Lounge would be Georgian in influence with a new chandelier in the center of the room weighing 1,800 pounds and designed and made especially for the lounge.

PROMENADE. As postwar prosperity grew, with the means to travel for both business and pleasure, people wanted comfortable rather than elegant lodgings when away from home. Remodeling the Mayflower to appeal to vacationing families and to the growing convention business became a priority. The gold leafing was covered, and the period furniture was sold. Additionally, the three main sculptures in the promenade were sold to the National Memorial Park Cemetery in Falls Church, Virginia.

AIR-CONDITIONING. One improvement of the Hilton era that was greeted with approval by hotel guests and visitors was the updating of the hotel air-conditioning system. No longer would only the public spaces by cooled by the old air-cooling system; now a new, modern system would cool them as well as the guest rooms against the hot Washington summers.

HILTON SPECIAL. In anticipation of the 25th anniversary of the Mayflower in 1950, the *Hilton Special* was chartered to bring Conrad Hilton and party to Washington, D.C. Hilton was guest of honor when General Manager C. J. Mack entertained at a large reception in the Grand Ballroom.

THE 25TH ANNIVERSARY CELEBRATION. Nicholas Marchitelli, executive chef; Anthony Macrello, night chef; Salvatore Mauizzo, chef garde-manger; Rudolph Langner, buffetier; Joseph Bastide, assistant buffetier; Mario Palmieri, chef confisseur; and Max Steiner, maitre d'hotel are pictured from left to right in a view of the Grand Ballroom and buffet before the beginning of the 25th anniversary reception. Both Hilton's portrait and a replica of the book *The Man Who Bought the Waldorf* were done in sugar.

THE CAKE. The birthday cake for the 25th anniversary was blue and silver surmounted by a replica of the Mayflower Hotel in white sugar. Around the foot of the cake were a few of the many floral arrangements sent by well-wishers commemorating the occasion.

INVITED GUESTS. A group of invited guests poses for pictures: from left to right they are Princess Wan Waithayakon, C. J. Mack, Conrad Hilton, and His Royal Highness Prince Wan Waithayakon (ambassador from Thailand). Prince and Princess Wan Waithayakon are just a couple of the many representatives of the international community in Washington, D.C., who attended the party. Overall 1,000 guests attended the party and were given a chance to meet the new owner, Conrad Hilton. He was quoted as saying that he meets "more interesting people in the Plaza in New York and the Mayflower in Washington than in any hotel he had ever purchased."

THE DAUGHTERS OF THE AMERICAN REVOLUTION. Genealogical-related societies, including the Daughters of the American Revolution (DAR) and the National Society of the Colonial Dames of America, began holding their national conventions at the Mayflower shortly after it opened. While the DAR no longer meets at the Mayflower, the National Society of the Colonial Dames of America and many others still do.

DAR LUNCHEON. The hotel staff would gear up for weeks prior to the Daughters of the American Revolution's arrival. There were general staff meetings to discuss the storage of the immense luggage and hatboxes the ladies would bring, the hotel silver was polished, and the fine china was readied for the ladies' tea service. The florist would create centerpieces using red, white, and blue flowers and provide orchid corsages.

DAR OVERFLOW. For years, the Daughters of the American Revolution was the biggest convention at the Mayflower, with attendance of over 1,400 ladies sometimes overflowing out in the Promenade in order to accommodate their large luncheons.

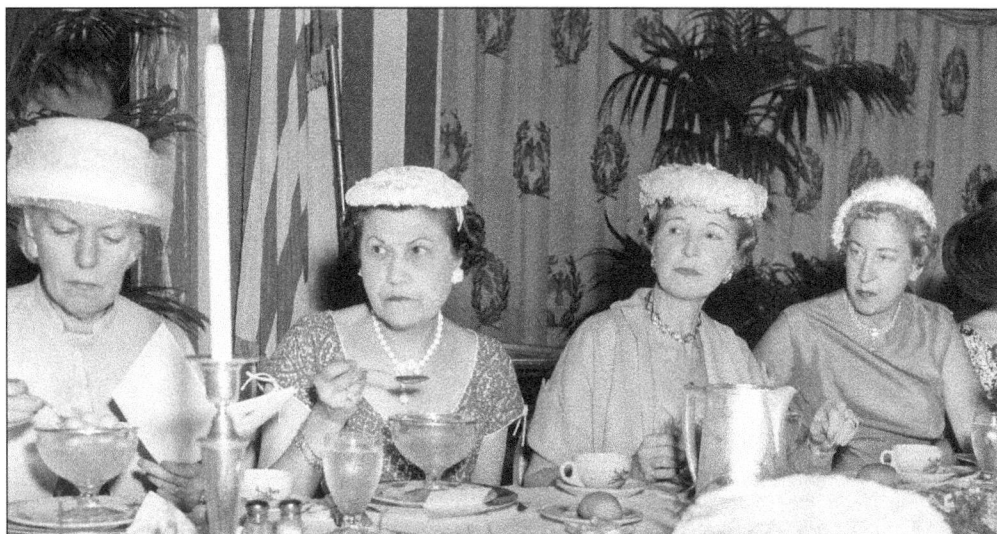

WOMEN'S PRESS CLUB LUNCHEON. Honorees at the 1956 Press Women of Washington Luncheon—hosted by the Pan American Liaison Committee on Women's Organizations and held in the Grand Ballroom—are, from left to right, Jean Eads, Violet Faulkner, Frances B. Applebee, and Betty Beale. At this time, the National Press Club did not admit women members.

DORIS FLEESON. The speaker at the Women's Press Club Luncheon was Doris Fleeson, who addressed "Women in a Changing World." Doris Fleeson was a newspaper reporter and syndicated columnist in Washington, D.C., for nearly 40 years, beginning in 1933, and was known as an aggressive political reporter. At one time, Fleeson was the sole permanent female member of the press entourage who accompanied President Roosevelt on his campaign tours.

KING OF MOROCCO, MOHAMMED V. In 1957, while visiting the United States, King Mohammed V hosted a dinner for President and Mrs. Eisenhower in the Grand Ballroom. Seen being escorted by General Manager C. J. Mack, the king was the Sulton of Morocco and successfully negotiated with France for the independence of Morocco. In 1957, he took the title of king.

PRESIDENT EISENHOWER. Seen being escorted by General Manager C. J. Mack, President Eisenhower arrives at the Mayflower to speak at the 1955 Conference of Governors in the Grand Ballroom. President and Mrs. Eisenhower attended many events at the Mayflower during their time in the White House.

PRAYER BREAKFAST. President Eisenhower speaks at the 1954 Prayer Breakfast in the Grand Ballroom. The breakfast was attended by Vice Pres. Richard Nixon, members of the president's cabinet, the Supreme Court, and 89 senators and 300 congressmen.

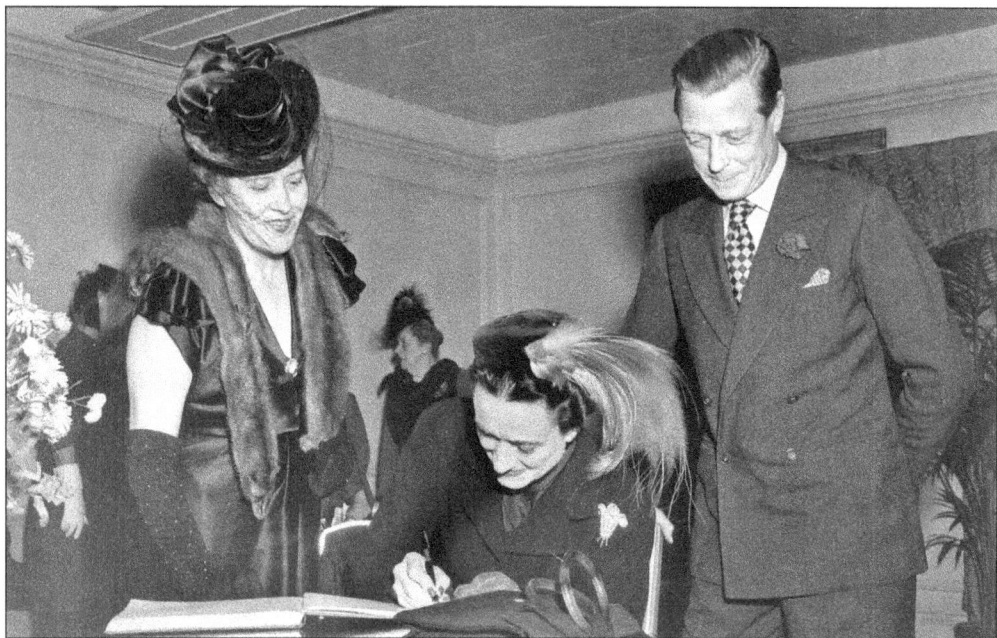

THE DUKE AND DUCHESS OF WINDSOR. While attending a luncheon hosted by the American Newspaper Women's Club, the Duke and Duchess of Windsor sign the Mayflower guest book. Margaret Hart, the society editor of the *Evening Star*, was their escort. The duke was the King of Great Britain, who abdicated the throne in ordered to marry American divorcée Wallis Simpson, causing a constitutional crisis in 1936.

BOB HOPE. While at the Mayflower, Bob Hope greets banquet manager Walter Seligman. Behind them is one of four James G. Tyler paintings in the Mayflower Hotel. There are two paintings that depict the Pilgrims' landing and two that show the *Mayflower* crossing. James G. Tyler was recognized as the premier marine artist of American and was more than 70 years old when the hotel opened.

PRESIDENT SUKARNO OF INDONESIA. President and Mrs. Eisenhower pose for photographers at the state dinner for President Sukarno of Indonesia in 1954. President Sukarno was the first president of Indonesia and helped the country win its independence from the Netherlands. During his presidency, he began to rely on the support of the Communist Party, increasing his ties to China and the aid of the Soviet bloc military. This aid, however, was surpassed by military support from the Eisenhower administration, which worried about the communist relationship.

EMPEROR HAILE SELASSIE I. Seen here greeting guests at a reception hosted by the Ethiopian Embassy is Emperor Haile Selassie. Because of its convenience to both the embassies located along Massachusetts Avenue and the White House, the Mayflower has been not only host to numerous state dinners but has also provided accommodations for visiting heads of state.

MAMIE EISENHOWER BIRTHDAY. In November 1954, nine hundred Republican women helped Mamie Eisenhower celebrate her 58th birthday. Television comedian Red Skelton was a surprise performer at the event—bursting out of a 7-foot-high birthday box. The women had an elaborate lunch followed by baked Alaska. The First Lady was presented with her own three-tier, white birthday cake.

YWCA 100TH BIRTHDAY. First Lady Mamie Eisenhower cuts the cake in the Grand Ballroom to celebrate the 100th birthday of the YWCA. The Women's Christian Association was formed in London in 1855. The YWCA USA is a women's membership movement based on the Christian faith and has a history of working toward the elimination of racism.

QUEEN ELIZABETH.
During her first visit to
the United States in 1957,
Queen Elizabeth passes by
the Mayflower Hotel on
Connecticut Avenue. She
would later return to the
hotel for a reception held
in the Grand Ballroom.
She also visited Jamestown,
Virginia, America's
first permanent English
settlement, to celebrate its
350th anniversary.

ROYAL THAILAND STATE DINNER. One of President Eisenhower's last events at the Mayflower was a state dinner in the Grand Ballroom given in his honor by Their Majesties King Bhumibol Adulyadej and Queen Sirikit of Thailand. The menu consisted of Hawaiian pineapple á la royale, lobster thermidor au four, heart of filet mignon grille rossnin with a perigourdine sauce, and white asparagus tips on lettuce with a vinaigrette sauce.

AUTO SHOW, 1958. Shortly after the Mayflower opened, retailers saw potential in the hotel's grand lobby and ballrooms for displaying their products. In 1938 and in subsequent years, General Motors and Chevrolet put several of their latest models on display at the hotel in the ballrooms.

GOLD SERVICE. The Mayflower's gold service set off the orchids in this display arranged by the hotel's own florists for the National Capital Flower and Garden Show in 1955. It took first prize in its category of cut flowers. The gold service and several other pieces were purchased at the estate sale of Evelyn Walsh McLean, a prominent hostess in Washington and the owner of the Hope Diamond.

RUSSIAN EMBASSY DINNER. In 1959, after a story reporting the details of the dinner planned at the Soviet Embassy by Premier Nikita Khrushchev for President Eisenhower appeared in the papers, the embassy relieved the caterer of all responsibility for the dinner. The Mayflower was then asked to provide the dessert, baked Alaska, and its complete gold service, linens, and a staff of 10 waiters and 2 captains for the function.

EASTER AT THE MAYFLOWER. The holidays have always been a time to celebrate and decorate the lobby area of the Mayflower. For years, Easter displays were created by the hotel floral department to the delight of young children visiting the hotel during this season.

CHRISTMAS AT THE MAYFLOWER. The Mayflower floral shop would always create elaborate displays for the holidays, with Christmas receiving most of their attention. Planning would begin months before when the theme and décor was selected. Overnight, the hotel would become a winter wonderland featuring a sled and reindeer in the center of the lobby and wreaths and garland hanging from the mezzanine level above.

CHERRY BLOSSOM FESTIVALS. The cherry blossom festivals have been held in Washington, D.C., since the 1930s. The National Cherry Blossom Festival annually commemorates the 1912 gift to the city of Washington of 3,000 cherry trees from Mayor Yukio Ozaki of Tokyo to enhance the growing friendship between the United States and Japan and celebrate the continued close relationship between our two peoples.

CHERRY BLOSSOM PRINCESSES. For many decades, the Cherry Blossom Queen was selected at an evening gala at the Mayflower Hotel. Here on the stage in the Grand Ballroom, the princesses await announcement of the Cherry Blossom Queen. Each of the representing states' names were placed on a wheel, and the queen was determined by the spin of that wheel.

CHERRY BLOSSOM QUEEN. Once selected, the queen's role was to preside over Cherry Blossom Festival events and to represent her state to national and international visitors and dignitaries throughout the year.

FASHION SHOWS. Beginning in the 1930s, the Connecticut Avenue Association held annual luncheon fashion shows at the hotel every spring and fall. Seen here during an Easter luncheon in the Grand Ballroom, the latest styles were shown to the approving crowd.

CLOTHING DISPLAY IN THE PROMENADE. Located on fashionable Connecticut Avenue, the Mayflower Hotel has been in a prime location to attract clothing retailers, which exhibit the latest fashions from local boutiques.

COFFEE SHOP. When it opened, the Mayflower Coffee Shop's walls were hung with landscapes of the Colonial period and the shop was a replica of "ye olde tyme coffee house." Service was quick, and special lunches were prepared for motorists and others to be taken from the hotel. Now modern to appeal to the taste of Washington the coffee shop would change again into the Rib Room.

PRESIDENT TRUMAN. A frequent guest at the Mayflower after leaving the White House, President Truman would sign the guest book as "Retired Farmer" under occupation. During one visit, a cashier new to the hotel did not recognize the former president and asked to see his credit card. He didn't have one, so she called the credit manager, who explained to her, "Presidents of the United States don't need credit cards."

DOORMEN. These are but two of the famous Mayflower doormen, Eddie Derendorf (left) and Bob Beavers. Eddie Derendorf, who retired after 47 years, said his favorite president was Harry Truman. The president and the doorman would walk around the block together for exercise, and on one visit, Derendorf rode with the former president in his limousine to Union Station. Bob Beavers was requested to be the doorman when Queen Elizabeth visited Washington, for Nikita Krushchev at the Russian Embassy, and was nicknamed the "Mayor of Connecticut Avenue."

THE SAPPHIRE ROOM. The modernization of the Garden Terrace resulted in this, the Sapphire Room, considered to be more in tempo with present-day tendencies of architects and decorators. Sparkling glass blocks and aluminum surfaces contrasted with the dominant blue color of the room and unnecessary ornamentation had been eliminated in favor of broad, plain areas. Work was carried out under the direction of Robert F. Beresford, original architect of the Mayflower. By all accounts, this design change did not last very long and the room was remodeled again.

THE WILLIAMSBURG ROOM. Now called the Williamsburg Room, this room's next change was more Colonial in design. The goal was to warm up the cold atmosphere of the Sapphire Room and to make the room appeal to the social groups utilizing the hotel during these years.

Five

A MODERN AND EFFICIENT MAYFLOWER
1960–1980

MAYFLOWER HOTEL. In 1956, to settle an antitrust suit filed against them, the Hilton Hotel Corporation sold the Mayflower and one of its New York hotels. The new owner was the Hotel Corporation of America (HCA) with A. M. Sonnabend as president of the purchasing company. The price was $12.8 million for the 1,000-room Mayflower Hotel. Hilton kept the newly constructed Hilton Statler on Sixteenth Street, now the Capital Hilton.

HOTEL LOBBY FACING THE PROMENADE. With plans to redecorate the lobby and continue the modernization begun by the Hilton Corporation, new owner the Hotel Corporation of American began their efforts of updating the Mayflower, enclosing the mezzanine level with wood paneling.

HOTEL LOBBY FACING THE FRONT DOORS. This area now became offices and shops instead of the once-elegant seating area. A drop ceiling was added that not only blocked the skylight but changed the overall appearance of the once-grand lobby. Carpet and a large fountain replaced the marble floor. The Mayflower now looked like any hotel in America.

LOBBY BAR. A new bar replaced a quiet sitting area in the lobby. The plaster relief of Ceres, the goddess of agriculture, and Bacchus, the god of wine, were covered. Gone were the antiques and sofas, to be replaced with modern leather chairs. While the *Mayflower* ship may have provided a backdrop for the bar, this no longer resembled the Mayflower Hotel that opened in 1925.

PROMENADE. The crystals were removed from the chandeliers, the artwork was removed from the walls, and the Mayflower Lounge was enclosed to create a new dining experience for hotel guests. No longer warm and inviting, the Promenade was stark and empty of all character and charm.

LIVING ROOM. The guest rooms were also updated during this time. Seen here is the living room of one of the suites or apartments. At the opening in 1925, each of the suites were custom designed with furniture selected individually for each apartment. These items were sold and replaced so that all rooms now looked alike.

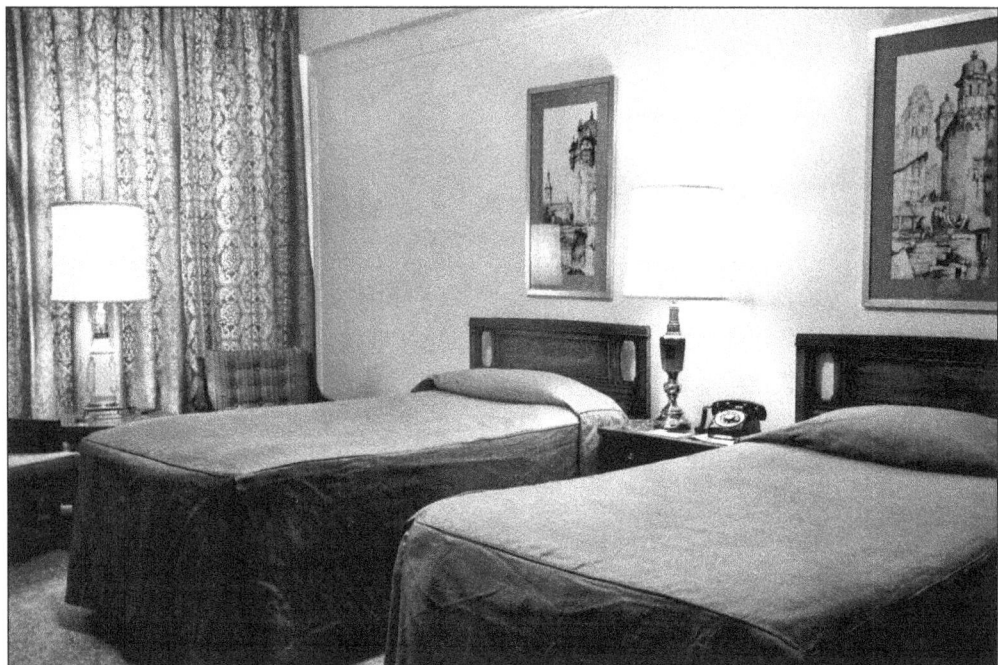

SLEEPING ROOM. Comfort and less style were the needs of this new era at the Mayflower. Features like televisions and even radio were required to keep pace with the newer, changing demand in hotels in the Washington area.

EAST ROOM. Luckily the ballrooms were pretty much left untouched during the modernizations of the 1960s. The Presidential Restaurant was converted into meeting and banquet space, as the hotel no longer required such a large dining room.

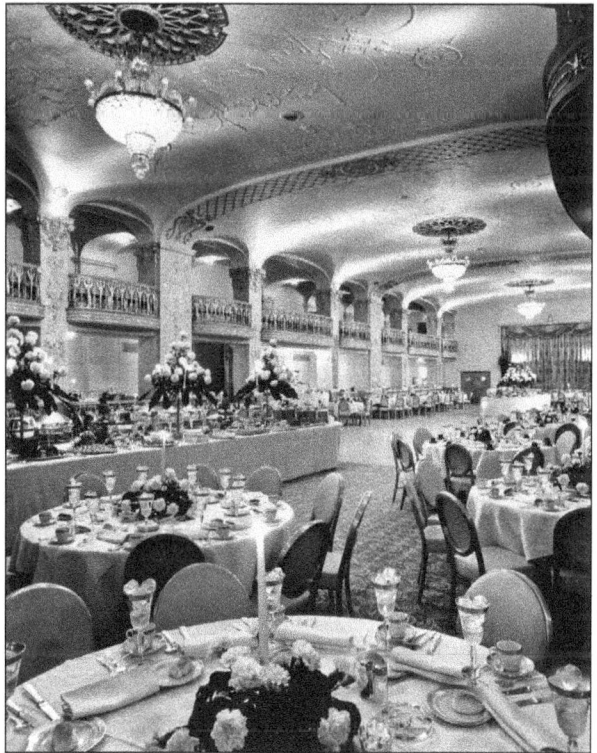

GRAND BALLROOM. The Grand Ballroom continued to be popular for events, and while most of the gold leafing was covered on the ceiling, it still was left with the relief work. Plans to enclosed the balconies and create a new presidential box never materialized, and the room continued to have much of the appearance it did when it hosted its first balls back in 1925.

SECOND-FLOOR MEETING ROOMS. New meeting rooms were carved out of former apartments and sleeping rooms on the hotel's second floor. These rooms were located in the former residences in the front of the hotel facing Connecticut Avenue and had names like Potomac, Concord, Columbia, District, and Capital.

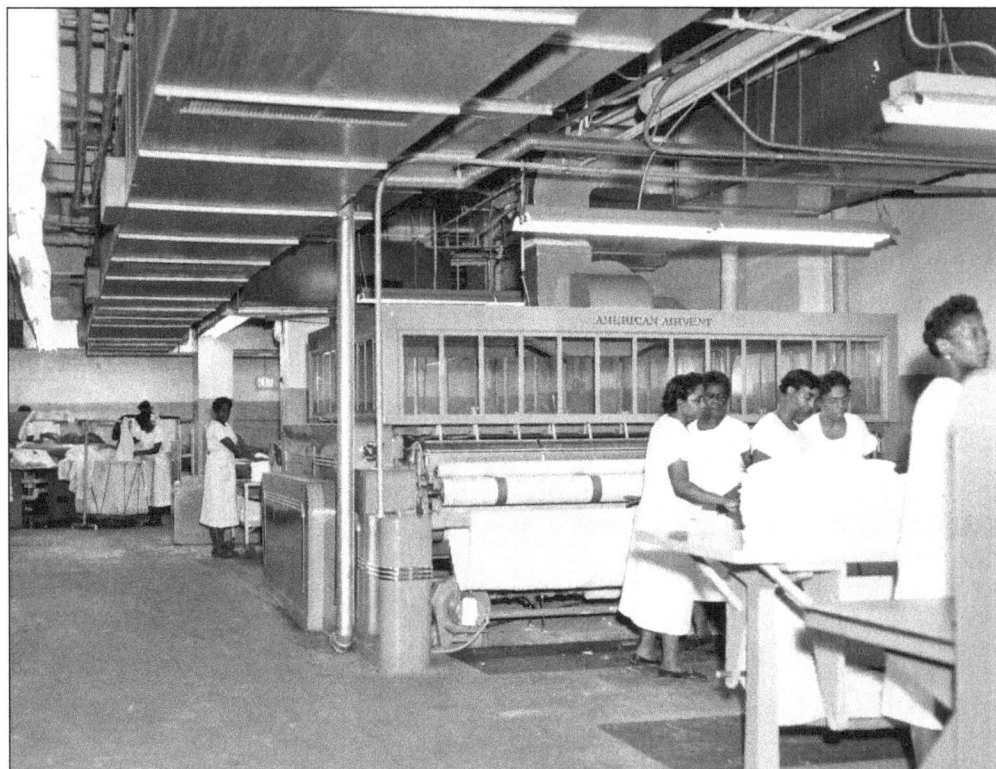

LAUNDRY. For over 30 years, the Mayflower handled all of its own laundering with a staff of 14 employees to supply the hotel with clean linen. The staff would feed an average of 12 sheets per minute into the presser. Finally in 1998, these services were sent off-site.

PRESIDENT AND MRS. KENNEDY.
The election of John F. Kennedy
brought with it a rash of inaugural
festivities to the Mayflower. In
addition to the inaugural ball,
Joseph P. Kennedy, the president's
father, hosted an intimate dinner
for 125 family members. Seen
here, Pres. John F. and Jacqueline
Kennedy enjoy a break in the
Promenade before returning to the
dinner in the Grand Ballroom.

KENNEDY INAUGURAL BALL. Just
hours before the Kennedy Inaugural
Ball, Washington was blanketed
with a blizzard that dropped 12
inches of snow, hampering most
travel. Here the President and Mrs.
Kennedy and Vice President and
Mrs. Johnson arrive at the Grand
Ballroom. In addition to the ball at
the Mayflower, President and Mrs.
Kennedy attended five other dances
at area hotels that night.

INTERNATIONAL VISITORS. Nigerian prime minister Abubkar Tafawa Balewa and his staff visited Pres. John F. Kennedy in July 1961 and attended a reception at the Mayflower Hotel held in their honor. The previous year, Nigeria gained independence from Great Britain and entered the United Nations as its 99th member.

PRESIDENTIAL PRAYER BREAKFAST. Vice Pres. Lyndon Johnson and the Reverend Billy Graham (center) share a moment before the 10th Annual Presidential Prayer Breakfast in 1962. The breakfasts were held in the Grand Ballroom at the Mayflower until they finally outgrew the space. The tradition of a Presidential Prayer Breakfast continues today in Washington, D.C., with President Bush speaking at the 55th annual breakfast in 2007.

PRESIDENT KENNEDY. President Kennedy would address several conventions at the Mayflower, including the Big Brothers of America, a dinner commemorating the 20th anniversary of the Truman Committee, a dinner given for members of Congress and administration leaders by the Democratic National Committee, the Business International Executive Roundtable, the White House Conference on Exports, and the American Bankers Association symposium on economic growth.

ROBERT KENNEDY. Seen in the Grand Ballroom, U.S. attorney general Robert F. Kennedy delivers a speech. After his brother's assassination in 1963, Kennedy continued as attorney general under President Johnson for nine months. In 1964, he was elected to the U.S. Senate from New York. In early 1968, Kennedy announced his own campaign for president but was assassinated in June of that year. To his right is Earl Warren, the 14th chief justice of the United States from 1953 to 1969. As chief justice, he swore in Presidents Eisenhower (second term), Kennedy, Johnson (full term), and Nixon (first term), and he also chaired the Warren Commission, which was formed to investigate the John F. Kennedy assassination.

J. EDGAR HOOVER. The former site of the hotel's coffee shop was later home to the Rib Room. Its most famous guest, FBI director J. Edgar Hoover, dined here nearly every working day for 20 years until his death in 1972. Sitting in his personal corner, where he would have his back to no one, he ordered the same meal everyday: chicken soup, buttered toast, and a salad of lettuce, cottage cheese, and grapefruit. He almost always brought his own diet salad dressing, which sometimes he would forget in the car and the wait staff would go and get for him. Hoover's waiter during the last eight years of his life was Joe Chapman. During his lifetime, his lunches at the Mayflower became so publicized that reporters would scout the hotel's main entrance and lobby, sometimes forcing him to slip out through the kitchen.

THE RIB ROOM. Opened in 1963 and later renamed the Carvery, the Rib Room was the third dining experience by this name opened in the Hotel Corporation of America chain. The lunch menu rotated on a 14-day cycle but "Roast Rib of Prime Prize Beef" was always on the menu. The restaurant had a seating capacity of 137 people.

LA CHATELAINE. The latest reinvention of the Mayflower Lounge in 1967 was the addition of La Chatelaine, "The Mistress of the Castle." It survived only six years but featured an atmosphere of medieval splendor and settees of orange velvet. The cuisine was international with an emphasis on the unusual and the spectacular, including a gong that announced the presentation of flaming food items. It was rated as one of the top restaurants in Washington, D.C.; however, it was finally closed and converted into banquet space to be called the Presidential Room.

JOHNSON INAUGURAL BALL. On the morning of January 20, 1965, the Johnson family attended an interdenominational church service led by the Reverend Billy Graham. Just after noon, Chief Justice Earl Warren administered the oath of office to Pres. Lyndon B. Johnson, and Johnson delivered his inaugural address. After a luncheon at the Capitol, the president viewed the Inaugural Parade. In the evening, the President and Lady Bird Johnson with Vice Pres. Hubert H. and Muriel Humphrey attended a Texas-style inaugural ball at the Mayflower Hotel.

JEAN DIXON. With a townhouse only a few blocks from the Mayflower, Jean Dixon (seated at right) was a regular at the Mayflower. Seen here with actress Arlene Dahl, she was one of the best-known American astrologers and psychics of the 20th century, thanks to her syndicated newspaper astrology column, some well-publicized predictions, and a best-selling biography.

JOHN WAYNE. Seen here enjoying lunch at the Mayflower is John Wayne. He was popularly known as the "Duke," as he epitomized rugged individualistic masculinity. Because of his enormous popularity, and his status as the most famous Republican star in Hollywood, the wealthy Texas Republican Party asked Wayne to run for national office in 1968, as had his friend and fellow actor, Sen. George Murphy. He declined, joking that he did not believe the public would seriously consider an actor in the White House.

GINGERBREAD HOUSE. For major holidays, the chefs of the Mayflower Hotel would create architectural confections for guests in the main lobby or for special events. In December 1964, famed pastry chef Manfred Prim created a 3-foot, 100-pound gingerbread house based on the story of Hansel and Gretel. The scene also featured two chocolate reindeer pulling Santa's sleigh. Prim's tasty creation won the "Artistic Individual Masterpiece Award" from the professionals at the Fifth Salon of Culinary Art. The gingerbread house was later given to the children at St. Ann's Infant Home.

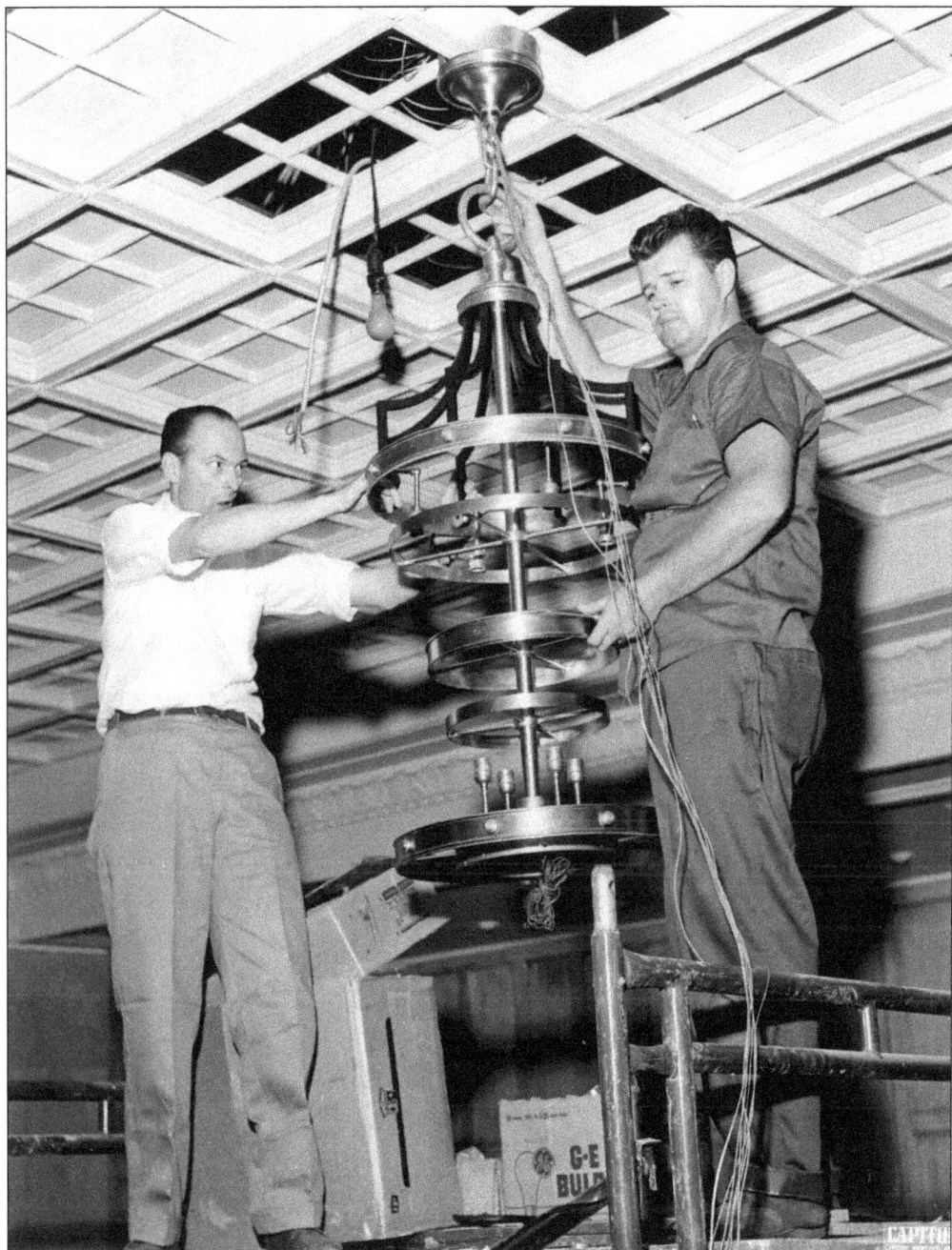

MORE CHANGES. In 1966, several newspapers reported that the Mayflower Hotel would undergo a $2.5-million remodeling project. Partially a reaction to the Hilton era, the work consisted of refurbishing 100 guest rooms and suites, redecorating several banquet halls, lighting updates, and redecorating the corridors of the guest areas.

ELECTION OF 1968. Vice Pres. Hubert Humphrey was running for U.S. president in 1968. In May of that year, he hired two jets to fly 162 Delaware delegates to the Mayflower Hotel for a lavish "thank you" reception. Nancy Sinatra serenaded the guests as they dined. On the night of the election, Humphrey and his supporters watched returns come in. It was a close election but one that he would lose. A few months later, the winner, Richard Nixon, celebrated his inauguration at the Mayflower Hotel.

NIXON INAUGURAL BALL. The election of 1969 brought the Republicans back into office, and President Nixon, who had been a constant visitor to the hotel during his early political career, returned for his inaugural ball in the Grand Ballroom. A specially built portico in the Grand Ballroom provides a stage from which the president could greet his guests. In 1974, the night before his resignation, Nixon would host a farewell for his staff at the Mayflower.

MAYFLOWER HOTEL. This concept shows the plans discussed during the 1971 construction of the Metro system in Washington, D.C. The plan was to tie the Mayflower Hotel to the nearby Metro station with a underground passage lined with retail shops. At that time, the hotel's 875-room count would have been reduced to 400 or 500 and the space converted to retail, a mall of about 150,000 square feet. At an estimated cost of over $8 million, not including any renovation to the hotel, the plan was deemed too expensive, and the Mayflower was saved.

SECRETARY OF STATE HENRY KISSINGER AND HUANG CHEN, CHIEF OF THE CHINESE DELEGATION. In 1973, President Nixon arranged for the United States to exchange diplomatic missions with the People's Republic of China. When the Chinese delegation arrived in Washington, their Embassy Row buildings were still being finished. The Mayflower played a role in international diplomacy by offering a wing of 12 rooms on the sixth floor as home for the 35 Chinese officials who set up a temporary liaison office as well as residence.

CHINESE DELEGATION. After their two-week stay was extended to eight months, the Mayflower planned a Wild West farewell party for the delegation, complete with cowboy hats, bandanas, and sheriff badges. Here General Manager Bill Hulett presents a model of the *Mayflower* ship to Ambassador Han Hsu of the People's Republic of China.

PRES. GERALD FORD. In September 1965, at a time when Gerald Ford's politic star was on the rise and Richard Nixon's had gone into political eclipse, the two men met for breakfast at the Mayflower Hotel to discuss rebuilding their damaged party. Seen here with General Manager Robert Wilhlem in 1975, Gerald Ford returned to the Mayflower as president of the United States after Richard Nixon's resignation. In 2007, the U.S. Army Military District of Washington and the White House travel staff would set up offices in the Cabinet Room to prepare for Ford's state funeral.

WALTER CRONKITE. Mike Lamber talks with CBS anchorman Walter Cronkite during the Democratic National Platform Committee meeting, held at the Mayflower, now a Westin Hotel, formally Western International. Lamber was the first general manager under this new management.

NELSON ROCKEFELLER. General Manager George DeKornfeld greets Nelson Rockefeller, former governor of New York and vice president, arriving at the Mayflower. Following President Nixon's resignation, new president Gerald Ford nominated Rockefeller to serve as the vice president, after a long process of considering various candidates. Rockefeller's top competition was George H. W. Bush.

CARTER INAUGURAL PARTY.
A crowd of 3,000 cheered when
President and Mrs. Carter
entered the Grand Ballroom of
the Mayflower during their 1977
inaugural party. Pres. Jimmy
Carter attempted to strip the
balls of their glitz and glamour
in 1977, calling them parties and
charging no more than $25 each.
New first lady Rosalynn Carter
even wore the same light-blue
chiffon dress that she had worn
to her husband's inauguration
as governor of Georgia in 1970.
The Carters stayed only for one
dance, to "Moon River."

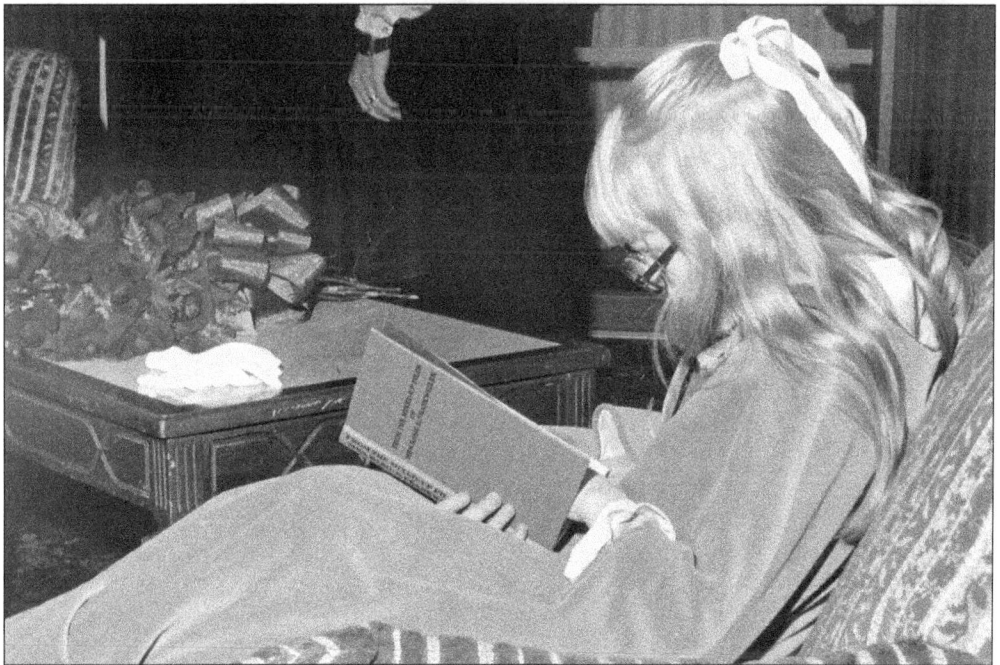

CARTER INAUGURAL PARTY. First Daughter Amy Carter reads a book borrowed from the White House library while her parents enjoy their inaugural party in the Grand Ballroom of the Mayflower.

MAYFLOWER CHEFS. During the signing of the peace treaty between Egypt and Israel, a state dinner was planned for 1,400 guests. The Mayflower chefs were asked to assist the White House kitchen in preparing the meal, as space in their kitchen was limited. Trays of cooked meat and tubs of sauces were packed into an insulated truck and sent to the White House. A thank-you letter read, "Although most of the guests were not aware of it, the dinner would not have been possible without the outstanding cooperation and assistance of the Mayflower staff to the success of this historic event."

Six

RESTORATION OF THE GRANDE DAME
1982–2006

FRONT OF HOTEL. In 1966, the Mayflower was purchased for $14 million by the May-Wash Associates. For the first time since it opened, the Mayflower was owned by local investors—Kingdon Gould Jr., William Cohen, Dominic Antonelli, and Ulysses Auger. By 1981, the Mayflower was a Stouffer Hotel, and plans were announced to restore the authenticity for which the Mayflower had been famous. May-Wash Associates released the following statement: "As owners, we are committed to the idea that the Mayflower Hotel must continue to be a significant asset to the city, and we will maintain for many years to come the standard of excellence for which it has been famous." They went to work and hired architects committed to blending new structural designs with the spirit and style of the original hotel.

EAST AND STATE ROOMS. Using old photographs, floor plans, and historic descriptions, work was begun to bring the hotel into present functionality, creating an aesthetic image faithful to the original conception of the Mayflower Hotel as envisioned by builder Allen Walker back in 1925.

CHANDELIERS RESTORATION. Chandelier expert David Toran reassembled and re-hung the six chandeliers that line the Promenade. Additionally, he would restore the chandelier in the hotel restaurant, the largest bohemian lead crystal chandelier in Washington. It was taken down and broken during renovation of the dome, the crystals were hidden inside an elevator well in the sub-basement, and the center shaft was finally found inside a dry storage room inside a cutout of solid wall that existed for unknown reasons. The chandelier was finally restored and reinstalled in 1991.

EDWARD LANING MURALS. During renovation of the restaurant, two large, Italianate-style murals were in danger of being ripped down. Long covered, the murals were later discovered to be the works of Edward Laning, a well-known Works Progress Administration (WPA) artist, and his assistant Philip Read. Hotel owners hired a painting conservator to treat the 1950s-era murals. Their existence came as a surprise to the art world and Laning scholars, who believed they were gone and were virtually unaware of their existence. Edward Laning was a member of the American Society of Painters, Sculptors, and Gravers. His work can be viewed at the Metropolitan Museum of Art, the Whitney Museum of American Art, the Smithsonian, and the New York Public Library. In addition, he created a mural for Ellis Island called the "Role of the Immigrant in Industrial America."

RESTORATION. After two years and at a cost estimated at $65 million, the restoration of the Mayflower Hotel was completed and the hotel was placed on the National Register of Historic Places, recognized as a significant building worthy of protection. Less than 10 years later, the hotel was added to the National Trust's Historic Hotels of America. The trust identified the Mayflower as a hotel that had faithfully maintained its "historic integrity, architecture and ambience."

GRAND BALLROOM. When the Mayflower opened, it was said the hotel had the most gold leaf of any Washington building after the Library of Congress. During restorations, the relief work was restored and some of the famous gold leaf was returned to the Grand Ballroom.

LOBBY. The lobby was retuned to its 1925 splendor, the frieze was uncovered, the marble columns with gold capital were restored, and the skylight was reopened, first blacked out during World War II and then covered with a drop ceiling in the 1960s. The railing around the mezzanine level was discovered in place; it had been used as support for the walls that once enclosed the space.

GOLD COLUMNS. The former site of office space, the mezzanine was reopened and converted back to its original use, as an open seating area for hotel guests to relax. The original capitals were one of the few features of the Mayflower destroyed by previous renovations. Using photographs and pieces of the original, they were re-created to appear the same as on opening day.

PROMENADE. The block-long promenade was the sight of the reopening celebrations, which included a parade from the Seventeenth Street entrance at the back of the hotel to the main lobby at Connecticut Avenue. During the ceremony, a congratulatory telegram was read from Pres. Ronald Reagan: "The Mayflower has been among the centerpieces of the social and political life of the nation's capital for more than half a century. It has housed important figures and hosted significant business, civil, political, government events."

CAFÉ PROMENADE. No longer dark and removed from the activities of the hotel, the restaurant was reopened to again look out onto the Promenade. The skylight, covered during World War II, was restored and reopened to flood light into the room. The chandelier was re-hung, and the room was returned to the quiet elegance for which it was famous.

POWER LUNCHEONS. At its opening in 1925, during Prohibition, the Palm Court was the tea room for the Mayflower Hotel and quickly after the repeal of Prohibition became the Mayflower Lounge. Today visitors come to the Mayflower to visit the Café Promenade for breakfast, lunch, dinner, and afternoon tea. The restaurant is the place of power luncheons attended by visiting senators and congressmen from Capitol Hill.

TOWN AND COUNTRY. An institution in itself, the lounge takes its name from the earlier Mayflower cocktail and snack lounge, the Town and Country Room, which opened in 1948 in the same spot. At opening, this was the site of the hotel pharmacy and later, after the repeal of Prohibition, the Men's Lounge. Today 101 martinis are on the menu.

NICHOLAS RESTAURANT. Nicholas Restaurant opened in November 1984 and was named for Mayflower chef Nicholas Marchitelli. The fine dining restaurant offered new American cooking served in an atmosphere of elegance, with seating for 92 and a private room for 10. The restaurant also had a private wine cellar with 7,000 bottles and 110 wines on the list. In the front of the hotel, along Connecticut Avenue, it was the site of the original hotel Coffee Shop and later the Rib Room and Carvery Restaurant. Nicholas closed in the early 1990s and is now retail space.

116

GRAND BALLROOM. Now fully restored, the Grand Ballroom has been for over 80 years the place to host a grand affair in Washington, D.C. Hundreds of brides and grooms cut their wedding cakes, thousands of debutantes made their formal bows, presidents and their first ladies danced at their inaugural balls, and people too numerous to count have been to lunches, dinner parties, graduations, charity balls, and other private celebrations in the Grand Ballroom. The site of Pres. Calvin Coolidge's 1925 charity inaugural ball, the Grand Ballroom continued to be a popular site for inaugural events for Democratic and Republican presidents alike, including Franklin Roosevelt, Harry Truman, Dwight Eisenhower, John Kennedy, Lyndon Johnson, Richard Nixon, Jimmy Carter, and Ronald Reagan, earning the Mayflower the title, "The Inaugural Ball Hotel."

CHINESE ROOM. What opened as a junior ballroom has become a popular and often requested space. The Chinese Room, named after the Oriental decor of the room, looks very much the same as in 1925. The dome, chandelier, and wall sconces are all original.

EAST AND STATE ROOMS. No longer the site of the hotel restaurant, these two rooms, which can be joined together, feature restored state seals around the perimeter of the room and two of the original four paintings—Thomas Jefferson and James Madison—from which the restaurant got its name.

COLONIAL ROOM. Located below the lobby, the Colonial Room has been one of the most changed spaces in the Mayflower. What began as a garden-themed Grille Room is now the Colonial Room. In 1994, during the baseball strike, owners and players met here to work out a resolution. While talks were progressing downstairs, President Clinton was attending his wife's Wellesley College reunion upstairs.

SECOND FLOOR. In August 1980, work began on the preliminary demolition of the 14 guest rooms on the eastern half of the second floor of the Mayflower. This area would become 12 new meeting rooms around two central foyers. The new second-floor meeting rooms were designed to provide a classic environment for small meetings and were added to meet the changing needs of the convention business that was becoming increasingly in demand.

GUEST ROOMS. Not much work was done to the exterior of the hotel, as it had essentially remained unaltered over the years. However, in the fall of 1981, construction would begin on the addition of the 9th and 10th floors on the rear of the hotel. At opening, the Mayflower front along Connecticut Avenue was 10 floors; however, the back of the hotel, mainly the apartment wing, was only eight stories. Also, during these renovations, the hotel's remaining guest room floors were completely rebuilt and redesigned.

LIVING ROOM OF SUITE. The last of the "Permanent Colony," as the residents were called, left the Mayflower just prior to the start of the restoration in 1980. What had been 112 multi-room apartments became one-bedroom suites for overnight guests. Designed in the style of the Federalist period with custom-designed Henredon pieces, what had been a 1,000-room hotel was now 657 sleeping rooms, each with the modern conveniences expected by the business traveler and vacationing families.

MAYFLOWER SUITE. During the renovation, two new luxury suites—the Mayflower Suite and the Presidential Suite—would replace the old Presidential and Vice Presidential Suites, not only in name but in location as well. These suites were rebuilt on the De Sales side of the hotel facing Connecticut Avenue and featured a foyer, living room, library, dining room, and two bedrooms.

FOYER OF PRESIDENTIAL SUITE. The entrance to the Presidential Suite on the 10th floor of the hotel features it own skylight with the seals of the 13 original colonies and the presidential seal in glass in the floor. During her deposition in the investigations conducted by Kenneth Starr, Monica Lewinsky stayed in this suite.

LIVING ROOM OF PRESIDENTIAL SUITE. Second Empire in design, the Presidential Suite has hosted many heads of state. Pres. Bill Clinton's mother, Virginia Kelley, and her husband, Dick, spent the night before her son's inauguration in the Presidential Suite at the Mayflower.

REAGAN INAUGURAL BALL. The Reagan Inaugural Ball was held at the Mayflower in 1981. The Pointer Sisters performed while the crowd of more than 3,500 overflowed into the Promenade. The Reagan Inaugural Ball was the last official inaugural ball held at the Mayflower.

PRESIDENT REAGAN. Seen here with Mayflower convention service director Jessie Smail, Pres. Ronald Reagan arrives at the Mayflower for his inaugural ball in 1981. In 2004, former aides and presidential library volunteers would return to the Mayflower and set up offices in the Cabinet Room to prepare and disseminate the 1,000 funeral invitations that Nancy Reagan wanted sent to family and friends during his state funeral. (Mattox Commercial photography, courtesy of Jessie Smail.)

BARBARA BUSH. Greeting First Lady Barbara Bush is General Manager Anthony Steward Moore as she arrives at the Mayflower, now a Stouffer-Renaissance Hotel. The Bush family is descended from Mayflower passengers John Howland, John Tilley, and Henry Samson.

PRES. GEORGE W. BUSH. General Manager Christian J. Mari greets Pres. George W. Bush who spoke to the American Enterprise Institute on the progress of Afghanistan and the Global War on Terror. Every U.S. president since Calvin Coolidge has been a guest at the Mayflower Hotel.

GOOD MORNING AMERICA. The morning after Pres. Bill Clinton's inauguration, ABC's *Good Morning America*, hosted by Charles Gibson and Joan Lunden, aired from the Mayflower Hotel on the mezzanine level.

PEACE LINKS. Peace Links established the Eleanor Roosevelt Living World Award for outstanding women in the cause of peace and conflict resolution. Recipients included Coretta Scott King, Rosalynn Carter, and Hillary Rodham Clinton. Pictured here (from left to right) at the Mayflower are Carol Williams, Peace Links, Elizabeth Callan Flanagan Bumpers (wife of former Arkansas governor and U.S. senator Dale Bumpers), Rosalynn Carter, Hillary Clinton, and Tipper Gore. (Mattox Commercial photography.)

PRESIDENT CLINTON. General Manager Anthony Steward Moore greets Pres. William Jefferson Clinton as he arrives at the Mayflower. (Mattox Commercial photography.)

FRONT OF HOTEL. Still the "Fifth Avenue of Washington," Connecticut Avenue in front of the Mayflower is no longer the quiet road it was in 1925 when the hotel opened. Today it is the busy crossroad of a modern city. The Mayflower, now a Renaissance Hotel, operated by Marriott Hotels, continues its place in history as host to presidents, foreign leaders, royalty, and Hollywood celebrities. The Mayflower Hotel is still the place where history is made in the nation's capital, the "Grande Dame of Washington, D.C."

Visit us at
arcadiapublishing.com

www.ingramcontent.com/pod-product-compliance
Lightning Source LLC
Chambersburg PA
CBHW050608110426
42813CB00008B/2494